Egypt, Greece, and Rome

Historical events literally took place in specific contexts; 'where things are' shapes 'how things are'. In this book, Corinna Rossi examines how three different ways of interacting with the surrounding world were shaped by their physical context in ancient Egypt, Greece, and Rome.

Following a discussion on the relationship between history and geography, Rossi delves into the geographical settings of these three civilisations, analysing human mobility within them and how cultural development was shaped by these movements. Rossi also identifies three possible models to describe the three different approaches specific to each of these ancient societies.

Egypt, Greece, and Rome: A History of Space and Places is suitable for students and scholars with previous understanding of these three civilisations and an interest in the relationship between history and geography.

Corinna Rossi is Associate Professor of Egyptology at Politecnico di Milano (Italy). She graduated in architecture in Napoli (Italy) and specialised in Egyptology at Cambridge (UK). She is the author of *Architecture and Mathematics in Ancient Egypt* and the co-author of *North Kharga Oasis Survey: Explorations in Egypt's Western Desert*.

Routledge Focus on Classical Studies

This new series, part of the Routledge Focus short-form programme, provides a venue for the most up-to-date research in the field of Classical Studies. The series covers a range of topics, from focussed studies on specific texts, figures, or themes, to works on wider issues.

Prophets, Prophecy, and Oracles in the Roman Empire
Jewish, Christian, and Greco-Roman Cultures
Leslie Kelly

Theophrastus' Characters
A New Introduction
Sonia Pertsinidis

Gallus Reborn
A Study of the Diffusion and Reception of Works Ascribed to Gaius Cornelius Gallus
Paul White

Democracies and Republics between Past and Future
From the Athenian Agora to e-Democracy, from the Roman Republic to Negative Power
Carlo Pelloso

Global Classics
Jacques A. Bromberg

Epic Echoes in *The Wind in the Willows*
Georgia L. Irby

Egypt, Greece, and Rome
A History of Space and Places
Corinna Rossi

For more information about this series, please visit: https://www.routledge.com/Routledge-Focus-on-Classical-Studies/book-series/FOCUSCLSS

Egypt, Greece, and Rome
A History of Space and Places

Corinna Rossi

LONDON AND NEW YORK

First published 2022
by Routledge
4 Park Square, Milton Park, Abingdon, Oxon OX14 4RN

and by Routledge
605 Third Avenue, New York, NY 10158

Routledge is an imprint of the Taylor & Francis Group, an informa business

© 2022 Corinna Rossi

The right of Corinna Rossi to be identified as author of this work has been asserted in accordance with sections 77 and 78 of the Copyright, Designs and Patents Act 1988.

All rights reserved. No part of this book may be reprinted or reproduced or utilised in any form or by any electronic, mechanical, or other means, now known or hereafter invented, including photocopying and recording, or in any information storage or retrieval system, without permission in writing from the publishers.

Trademark notice: Product or corporate names may be trademarks or registered trademarks, and are used only for identification and explanation without intent to infringe.

British Library Cataloguing-in-Publication Data
A catalogue record for this book is available from the British Library

Library of Congress Cataloging-in-Publication Data
A catalog record has been requested for this book

ISBN: 978-1-032-18599-6 (hbk)
ISBN: 978-1-032-18601-6 (pbk)
ISBN: 978-1-003-25531-4 (ebk)

DOI: 10.4324/9781003255314

Typeset in Times New Roman
by Deanta Global Publishing Services, Chennai, India

Σοφίᾳ καὶ Εἰρήνῃ

Contents

List of figures	ix
Foreword	x
Acknowledgements	xiii
Note on transcriptions and translations	xiv

Introduction   1
 Bibliographical references 4

1 Limits   5
 Definitions 5
 Connections 15
 Bibliographical references 22

2 Ancient Egypt   27
 Places and cycles 27
 Water and sand 37
 Division and unification 43
 Bibliographical references 48

3 Ancient Greece   54
 Size and identity 54
 Travelling by sea 69
 Dots and lines 75
 Bibliographical references 82

4 Ancient Rome 87
Expansion 87
Travelling by land 97
Keeping the empire 106
Bibliographical references 112

5 Recontextualisations 116
Transmissions 116
History, space, and places 120
Bibliographical references 124

Index 127

Figures

1.1	Timeline	16
1.2	Concept map	21
2.1	Physical map of Egypt, from Google Earth	28
2.2	The territory of ancient Egypt (1): from left to right, the Valley and the territorial extent of the proto-states (3500–3000 BCE), of the Old Kingdom (2686–2181 BCE), and of the Middle Kingdom (2055–1650)	29
2.3	The territory of ancient Egypt (2): from left to right, the Valley and the territorial extent of the New Kingdom (1550–1077) and of the Ptolemaic period (305–30 BCE)	30
3.1	Physical map of Greece, from Google Earth	55
3.2a	Phoenicial cities (empty circles) and progressive expansion of Greek cities: II millennium (empty stars), I millennium (stars), and VIII century BCE (squares)	58
3.2b	VII century (triangles), VI century (circles), V century (vertical losanges) and IV century BCE (horizontal losanges)	59
3.3	*Combined* view of Phoenician cities, Greek cities and their colonies from the II millennium to the IV century AD	60
3.4	The western portion of the Persian Empire and the Greek *poleis*	65
3.5	Coastal maritime routes according to the *periplous* of Pseudo-Scylax (thicker line), with connectivity among Aegean islands highlighted (broken lines)	72
4.1	Physical map of the territory under Roman rule, from Google Earth	88
4.2a	Progressive expansion of the Roman territory: 700 and 500 BCE	92
4.2b	The Roman territory in 240 and 60 BCE	93
4.3	Maximum extent of the Roman Empire in AD 117	94
4.4	Simplified map of the main roads crossing the Roman Empire. The thicker line represents the *Itinerarium Antonini*	99
5.1	Mega-place, para-place, and meta-place	123

Foreword

> The difference between a historian and a poet is not that one writes in prose and the other in verse-indeed the writings of Herodotus could be put into verse and yet would still be a kind of history, whether written in metre or not. The real difference is this, that one tells what happened and the other what might happen. For this reason poetry is something more scientific and serious than history, because poetry tends to give general truths while history gives particular facts. By a 'general truth' I mean the sort of thing that a certain type of man will do or say either probably or necessarily. That is what poetry aims at in giving names to the characters. A 'particular fact' is what Alcibiades did or what was done to him.
>
> (Arist. *Poet.* 1451b)

In order to understand the past, to grasp the development of ancient civilisations, we feel the need to define time and space. We wish to describe the succession of events within the place and period in which they took place as a fundamental tool for a correct historical epistemology. One might wonder, though, whether our etic approach leads to a better understanding of the ancient perception of these two variables (Clarke 1968).

Herodotos, considered the 'Father of History', uses for the first time the word 'historia' indicating his investigation of the past. In searching for the reason for the contrasts that led to the Persian Wars, he studies what we now consider historical as well 'mythical' events. One generation later, Thucydides, in his introduction, starts from the Trojan War. We might be surprised that an analysis of the past includes episodes we classify as 'non-historical': the role and function of Agamemnon and other heroes of the Trojan War had a value without being placed in a definite time and space (Finley 1975: 5–36). In this respect, Hans Meyerhoff noted that past generations knew less of the past compared to us, but they preserved a sense of identity and continuity with it (Meyerhoff 1955: 109).

As a direct consequence we should be careful in defining what we might consider historical sources. In ancient Egypt one would start for sure from Royal Annals and king lists. We should include royal accounts of military victories, building projects, and private inscriptions, too. One should be aware, though, that what, according to us, are records of historical events, to ancient people 'were simply instruments of thanksgiving or a promise of additional offerings' (Leprohon 2020: 973). So many of the events listed in these texts are of a cultic nature. At the same time useful information 'to reconstruct history' can be found in mythological tales. In fact, although these texts do not report any recognisable historical episode, they convey ideas related with the state and can shed light on the activity of the king. So, for instance, the *Story of Sinuhe* is still the only source that we have that might allude to the assassination of Amenemhat I and it gives a clear picture of Middle Bronze Age Western Asia, while the trip of Wenamun to the Levant shows the decline of Egypt's influence in the region (Leprohon 2020: 973). In the Middle Kingdom *Tale of the Shipwrecked Sailor*, the description of a 'magical space', a 'supernatural island', conveys the Egyptian perception of the unknown and of the force of nature.

Religious texts are of clear interest to understand the ancient Egyptian idea of the physical space within which life can develop. The *Amduat* is generally regarded as the earliest example of a new genre, the *Books of the Netherworld*, all of which present the world beyond in a combination of text and pictures. These *Books of the Afterlife* provide the royal deceased with the knowledge necessary to survive in the company of the Gods. The New Kingdom religious cosmographies are not composed of variable collections of spells like the *Pyramid Texts*, the *Coffin Texts* or the *Book of the Dead*, but they have permanent, unchanging contents. Their pictures are not separate vignettes but they form a solid unity with the text. Rows of deities and symbols usually stand on their own in the other corpora, whereas the scenes in the *Books of the Afterlife* are accompanied by a text describing the actions of the figures involved (Hornung 1999: 26–7; Hoffmann 1996: 26–40).

Thus, texts and pictures in the *Books of the Afterlife* have complementary roles. The image would represent what could not be expressed in words, while abstract concepts, which could not be represented in a picture, were described in words (Brunner 1980: 219). The iconographic depictions support different statements at the same time: image and text constituted the systems of representation of the mythical space where the sun could carry out his journey. In other words, the *Books of the Afterlife* described, organised, and expressed the Egyptian comprehension of the universe (Brunner 1979: 212–3; Tefnin 1984: 55; Assmann 1987: 40).

Only by combining history, mythology, and theology, can we thus aim at understanding how time and space were perceived. In order to achieve this result, we have to go beyond the disciplinary borders of history and geography: the combination of a bird's-eye view with a close-range perspective may allow us to reconstruct the ancient landscape that witnessed the sequence of events that took place in the ancient world.

Christian Greco

Bibliography

Primary sources

Arist., *Pol.*: Aristoteles, *Politica*. English translation from the Perseus Digital Library (perseus.tufts.edu).

Secondary sources

Assmann J. 1987. 'Hierotaxis: Textkonstitution und Bildkomposition in der altägyptischen Kunst und Literatur', In J. Osing and G. Dreyer (eds.), *Form und Mass. Festschrift für Gerhard Fecht*. Wiesbaden, Harrassowitz: 18–42.
Clarke D. 1968. *Analytical Archaeology*. London, Methuen.
Brunner H. 1979. 'Illustrierte Bücher in alten Ägypten', In H. Brunner, R. Kannicht, and K. Schwager (eds.), *Wort und Bild*. Munchen, Wilhelm Fink.
Brunner H. 1980. 'Unterweltsbücher in ägyptischen Königsgräbern', In G. Stephenson (ed.), *Leben und Tod in den Religionen. Symbol und Wirklichkeit*. Darmstadt, Wiss. Buchgesellschaft: 201–08.
Finley M. I. 1975. *The Use and Abuse of History*. London, Chatto and Windus.
Hornung E. 1999. *The Ancient Egyptian Books of the Afterlife*. Ithaca/London, Cornell University Press.
Hoffmann N. 1996. 'Reading the Amduat', *Zeitschrift für Ägyptische Sprache* 123: 26–40.
Leprohon R. J. 2020. 'Historical Texts', In I. Shaw and E. Bloxam (eds.), *The Oxford Handbook of Egyptology*. Oxford, Oxford University Press: 971–93.
Meyerhoff H. 1955. *Time in Literature*. Berkeley/Los Angeles, University of California Press.
Tefnin R. 1984. 'Discours et iconocité dans l'art Egyptienne', *Göttinger Miszellen* 79: 55–69.

Acknowledgements

The first person that I must thank is Serafina Cuomo, who read an early version of the text. Without her precious advice not only on the sources to be consulted but also on the overall meaning and structure of this work, this book would have never been written. Later versions benefited from the vast expertise of Roger Bagnall, who made important suggestions to sharpen the focus of the research, and Paola Davoli, who suggested further lines of investigations. I wish to thank the anonymous reviewers, who provided extremely useful comments to address the last phase of review of the text.

In the final stages of the work, Alessandro Mandelli and Cinzia Tommasi patiently turned my thoughts into images, while Nicoletta De Troia provided a final check on the consistency of terminology and translations. I am grateful to Amy Davis-Poynter, Marcia Adams and Sushmitha Ramesh at Routledge for skillfully steering me through the publishing process.

I would also like to thank the European Research Council, in particular Manfred Bietak and the entire panel of the 2015 Consolidator Grants, chaired by Katerina Harvati-Papatheodorou. Even if this work is not the direct output of my ERC-funded project LIFE, it would have never been completed without the professional stability and the stimulating academic environment that derived from the grant that I was so lucky to be awarded. Thanks are therefore also due to the Department ABC of Politecnico di Milano (Italy) that took me onboard, and in particular to Stefano Della Torre, who opened the way for me.

Last but not least, I would like to thank Christian Greco, who encouraged me on countless occasions to pursue my path, more certain of its value than I am.

Note on transcriptions and translations

In order to enhance the readability of the text, I adopted a combination of criteria: I used simplified transcriptions, generally retaining the Greek spelling but favoured in some cases the most common version of the names of people and places. The abbreviations are those of the Oxford Classical Dictionary, and most of the translations come from sources accessible from the web.

Introduction

The idea of writing this book was born in the Egyptian Western Desert. My archaeological work at the remote site of Umm al-Dabadib, in the Kharga Oasis, year after year, took me to the edges of what still is the inhabitable world. The site is totally isolated and has seen very little activity since the Late Roman period; out there, there is no water, no road, no electricity, no mobile phone network. When I go there, I travel back in time from modern Italy to ancient Roman Egypt, following backwards also the history and evolution of travelling: a large and well-equipped airplane takes me and all my luggage to Cairo, and a smaller one south to Luxor; a well-worn 4x4 takes me (and my luggage) across 350 km of desert to the oasis and finally, on the following day, to Umm al-Dabadib. If I want to reach the upper edge of the imposing system of underground aqueducts that served the settlement and its vast agricultural system, I must then leave the car and walk for 3 km along a *wadi* filled by barchan dunes, with the bare minimum packed in a small backpack on my shoulders. In four days I go back sixteen centuries, and I end my journey walking.

Whenever new members join the team on the field, I always take them to the northern edge of the site, where the Roman aqueduct starts: only when you reach that point, after two hours spent climbing rocks and dunes, baked by a scorching sun or battered by strong sand-laden winds, do you understand the effort that the ancients made, and therefore the actual size, value, and importance of the site which is the object of our studies.

In the evening, sitting on the top of the dune that hosts our camp of tents in its hollow, I started wondering how our modern and relatively effortless way of travelling affects our understanding of events that belong to a past when the conditions in which people interacted with the surrounding territory were significantly different. I was offered the chance to organise my thoughts on the occasion of a course that I taught at Bocconi University in 2010, and in a subsequent series of seminars at the Fondazione Collegio delle Università Milanesi in 2013; some aspects are now incorporated into

DOI: 10.4324/9781003255314-1

my current courses at Politecnico di Milano. The positive response of the students on all these occasions convinced me to start organising this experience in writing. The project remained latent for a while, until it found new inspiration from the collaboration with the research activities promoted by Museo Egizio, Torino. The work carried out in preparation for the exhibition *Archeologia Invisibile* (Greco 2019) prompted further reflections on the role of the context in archaeology, which concerns objects of any size, from small finds to buildings, to entire settlements.

Of course, the result is a faulty book. It mirrors my personal knowledge on a complex combination of subjects, and is therefore bound to be uneven, incomplete, and at times perhaps depthless. In order to partly justify my obstinacy in publishing it, I would like to stress that its aim is not to produce a panoramic view over the three cultures mentioned in the title, but rather to offer the chance to adopt a slightly different perspective when looking back at historical events. This book is meant for readers who already have a general knowledge of the ancient Egyptian, Greek, and Roman cultures; it does not provide a general historical framework and does not pretend to be exhaustive. It may be described as a spotlight pointing from a new direction towards a complex combination of objects, accompanied by a select bibliography containing clues to expand one's curiosity in various directions.

The starting point is the request to the reader to forget our modern way of experiencing and moving across the environment that surrounds us. In the last century, technological development has radically changed the way in which many people travel. The spread of motorised vehicles represented a first giant leap; now nearly ubiquitous, they deeply modified the way in which people move around on a daily basis. Another major revolution was represented by the development of civil aviation, which nowadays allows a large number of people to reach distant destinations in a very short time. In many countries, commuters take for granted being able to cover every day an amount of kilometres that 200 years ago would have required weeks – not to mention the distances that we happily cover to go on holiday.

In general, it takes an erupting volcano or a major storm to remind us that we cannot always cross our continents in a few hours, exactly when and how we planned to do. An increasingly larger number of modern travellers can afford to ignore the territory across which they move: tunnels pierce high mountains, bridges cross large rivers, planes fly over everything. Departure point and destination are the only important data for someone who boards a plane or a train; what lies in between is irrelevant (cf. Geertz 1996: 262). Google Earth, finally, allows anyone endowed with a web connection to virtually fly and land anywhere (to be precise: in any place that has been thoroughly documented through images), thus bringing the dematerialisation of travelling to the extreme.

Until about 150 years ago, however, things were significantly different: travellers walked or rode along a loose network of unpaved roads, used a limited number of bridges to cross rivers and crevices, climbed high mountain passes, and spent long weeks or even months at sea to reach the most distant destinations. Travelling, including transporting goods and information, meant negotiating with territory and weather conditions in a physical and direct way, and could be altogether a rather difficult and dangerous enterprise. This is still true, of course, in many parts of the world; a growing number of people, however, can afford to forget about it.

Sometimes, something reminds you of how things actually worked in the not-so-distant past. I will never look again at an object made of red porphyry without a shiver: I still remember how much it took to climb the unstable slope covered by loose stones that leads to the Roman quarry, located on a high peak in the heart of Egypt's Eastern Desert. And I had reached the base of the mountain well settled in a comfortable 4x4, not dragging myself along miles and miles of unpaved roads.

Stating that different environments shape different cultures may sound obvious, but sometimes we tend to forget what this really meant in practical terms. The modern, slightly scornful approach to the ancient (and not-so-ancient) obsession about the influence of the environment on human bodies and minds, after all, has grown in progression together with the improvement of our living conditions: it is easy, now, to dismiss the claims of the author of *De aere, aquis et locis* from an air-conditioned office that has been effortlessly reached by public or private transport on wheels or rails. To this we may add the progressive detachment of our attention from some of our physical abilities, fuelled by the growing role of technology in the life of an increasing number of people: GPS navigators are trusted more than written signs on the roads, and the problem of avoiding picking up poisonous food is absent from the mind of those who shop in supermarkets (Harari 2018: 88–9).

The increasing role of GPS positioning systems surreptitiously introduced in the daily life of smartphone users a type of knowledge and an amount of interconnected information which one would never be able to acquire at ground level, and that is now taken for granted. You can literally ask your phone where you (both) are, and it will respond. Its reply will refer to your position in the *space* mapped by satellites, and only as a by-product may it (or may it not) be able to tell you something of the *place* where you find yourself.

Going back to Umm al-Dabadib and the Kharga Oasis, I made and make extensive use of satellite images to study the shape and distribution of the Late Roman settlements and investigate their historical role on the basis of their geographical position. This approach has been gaining importance, especially in the last few years, when the security of the Western Desert worsened and fieldwork had to be interrupted. Using Google Earth seated at my desk, surrounded by my books, indifferent to the weather conditions outside the window, has helped me to grasp the big picture that I could not see during the fieldwork, when I had to negotiate with my physical ability, strength, and patience to walk under the sun, crawl along the stairs of the Fort and wait for the periodic sandstorm to go away. These two points of view offer the chance to see the same object (the archaeological site) from two different perspectives, which complement each another.

For a long time, the working title of this book was *How Geography Shaped History*: in a nutshell, this is the quickest way to describe the essence of the following pages. However, I eventually felt that the core issue here was not the relationship between these two disciplines, but rather how, in Antiquity, elements nowadays pigeonholed in one of these two disciplines mixed and combined with one another.

In this book, I will try to alternate and combine, in metaphorical terms, the two views described above: the detached and dematerialised sight from the satellite (the space) and the subjective, practicality-bound perspective from ground level (the place), to remind and remember that behind every line drawn on a map, there was someone who walked that distance (cf. Malpas 2018: 37–9).

This is a journey on paper to the beginning of the aqueducts of Umm al-Dabadib.

Bibliographical references

Geertz C. 1996. 'Afterword', in S. Feld and K. H. Basso (eds.), *Senses of Place*. Santa Fe, School for Advanced Research Press: 259–62.

Greco C. 2019. 'The Biography of Objects', *The International Archives of the Photogrammetry, Remote Sensing and Spatial Information Sciences* XLII-2/W11: 5–10.

Harari N. Y. 2018. *21 Lessons for the 21st Century*. London, Jonathan Cape.

Malpas J. 2018. *Place and Experience: A Philosophical Topography* (2nd edition). London, Routledge.

1 Limits

> As for Ocean, the Greeks say that it flows around the whole world from where the sun rises, but they cannot prove that this is so.
>
> (Hdt. 4.8)

Definitions

Geography and history

The relationship between geography and history has been the subject of discussions for a long time. Although it is generally agreed that 'history is not intelligible without geography' (George 1901: 1), how geography and history interact, overlap, or even coincide is a matter of debate.

As Clarke summarised, two main models emerged from the discussion: one attributing geography to the realm of space and history to that of time, and another associating geography to the present and history to the past. The first suggests a separation between space and time that is difficult to maintain, as 'geography and history both require a spatial and a temporal context' and, moreover, does not take into account the 'experienced space' (Clarke 1999: 4ff, esp. 6–8; see also Merrills 2005: 8–9). The present–past model, summarised by the sentence 'the geography of the present day is but a thin layer that even at this moment is becoming history' (Darby 1953: 6) is challenged by the observation that 'just as history is not entirely concerned with the past, so it is hard to envisage a geography that deals exclusively with the present' (Clarke 1999: 16).

The heated debate that took place on this subject in the middle of the last century was addressed by Baker in his book *Geography and History*, bearing the revealing subtitle *Bridging the Divide* (2003). The interconnections that can be established between these two disciplines are illustrated in his first figure, a diagram showing how their overlap produces the mirroring pairs of 'history of geography' and 'geography of history' on the

DOI: 10.4324/9781003255314-2

one hand, and 'historical geography' (the historical dimension in geography) and 'geographical history' (the geographical dimension in history) on the other hand. Baker highlighted that 'geography and history are different ways of looking at the world but they are so closely related that neither one can afford to ignore or even neglect the other' (2003: 3). This may offer a conciliatory conclusion to a number of current discussions, but does not necessarily help in the investigation of how geography and history were related in the past, when their perception and definitions were different.

Modern geography is a complex interdisciplinary field, constructed over a long period of time by the progressive combination of physical, human, cultural, and economic components (Agnew and Livingstone 2011: 1–3). The relatively recent development of science and technologies created new directions of research that generated specific definitions (cf. Curry 2005); if some of them strictly depend on modern methods and tools, the seeds of others can be traced back to Antiquity. In this respect, we can often look back in time and follow backwards the steps that led to the development of modern disciplines, and thus gain a historical perspective linking past and present.

On the other hand, gaining a historical perspective works, by definition, only backwards, as every given moment of the past was once present, with no visibility on future developments and often with little or no awareness of the big picture. This individual, partial, and biased perception of the situation may be paired to the 'ground-level view'. When we look back to past events, we can afford instead to rise above the current circumstances and look at them in perspective from a privileged point of view, unsurprisingly defined 'bird's-eye view'.

When we study ancient Egypt, Greece, and Rome, or any other ancient civilisation, we obviously apply a variable combination of these two points of view, using what we have learned over the centuries to reconstruct what our ancestors did and thought. Keeping a balance between the two approaches is not easy, and in fact we often make the mistake of attributing intentions *ex post*, especially when we move within what we today classify as the 'scientific' realm.

As Casey noted (1996: 35), 'all human beings may desire to know, but they do not always desire to know in the foundationalist manner that is an obsessive concern of European civilization'. Bearing this in mind, in this book I will use the work 'geography' in its literal, etymological meaning of description (*graphia*) of the Earth (*ge*). To be precise, a more articulated translation of *graphia* would be 'description by means of lines', thus including both written and drawn descriptions. I will then split the *geo-graphia* into two descriptions, the bird's-eye and the ground-level view. The former corresponds to the attempt to grasp the big picture and somehow harness and codify it by means of a shared reference grid. The latter corresponds to the physical and personal experience of interaction with the local landscape and environment. In other words, the former corresponds to a description of the space, the latter to the description of a place.

If we look back at ancient Greece, at the 'origins' of our concepts of history and geography, drawing a precise line dividing the two fields is not a simple task. As Clarke summarised, in the Hellenistic period 'we have evidence for separate geographical and historical works (...). But the contents, organizing principles, and character of these works are often very similar'. For instance, a common problem was to establish shared reference points: just as spatial grids could be based on some physical points, the Olympiads started to act as reference dates to impose a coordinated time-system. History and geography, as we define them now, are deeply intertwined in the works of Herodotos and Polybius. Strabo wrote both a 'Geography' (*Geographika*, that survived) and a 'History' (*Historika Hyponmemata*, 'historical sketches', now lost); if both had survived to us, we would probably have a better idea of how the two subjects were perceived and identified in comparison with each another (Clarke 1999: 2, 11–4, 26, 344).

Some form of 'geographical thinking' (an awareness of the different environmental conditions into which people lived) certainly existed long before it was codified by the Greek polymath Eratosthenes in the III century BCE (Holt-Jensen 2018: 21; Geus 2018; see also Agnew and Livingstone 2011: 27 and 33–5 and Casey 1996: 20). The terms *geographia* and *geographos* (geographer) come from the verb *geographeo*, 'to describe the earth', probably by analogy with the verb *geometreo*, 'to measure the earth'. Both *geometria* and *geographia* evolved into scholarly disciplines; whereas, the older *kosmographia*, the 'description of the world' (possibly the title of a now-lost work by Democritus of Abdera, dating to the V century BCE), fell into oblivion and was replaced by the more successful term *geographia* (Roller 2010: 1–2).

Eratosthenes, in his role of librarian at Alexandria, had access to all the most relevant sources on the known world that had been collected by that time (the III century CE), including the fresh survey of the route running along the Nile from Alexandria to Syene (modern Aswan) to Meroe (in modern Sudan). These measurements represented the basis for his calculation of the circumference of the Earth, which earned him notoriety as a mathematician; of this treatise, *Peri tes anametreseos tes ges* ('On the Measurements of the Earth'), only fragments survive. He then moved to the description of what was on the Earth and wrote his *Geographika* by combining astronomical data with travellers' reports, a method that was later criticised by Hipparchos and others (Roller 2010: 31 and Appendix 1).

It is interesting to note that Eratosthenes, often called the 'Father of Geography', was not interested in fieldwork and wrote his *Geographika*

8   *Limits*

based on other people's accounts; by contrast, Herodotos, commonly identified as the 'Father of History', based his *Historiai* (to be properly translated as 'investigations', written in the V century BCE) on his personal observations, collected during his extensive travels (Roller 2010: 17; see also Thomas 2000; Hartog 1988; Schepens 1980). In both cases, it is clear that the growing interest in the surrounding world was directly related to the increasing number and extent of travels, and to the ensuing knowledge that kept accumulating at a fast pace (Casson 1994). That the geographical knowledge was linked to the possibility of establishing contacts with local populations is indirectly testified later also by Strabo, uninterested in territories that were uninhabited (Clarke 1999: 29).

By the late Hellenistic period, Eratosthenes' topographical data referring to the western portion of the Mediterranean were considered obsolete; and by the time Strabo wrote his *Geographika* (the I century CE) the westward expansion of Roman interests had greatly increased the knowledge of coasts and lands that were little known to the earlier Greek travellers, more focused on the eastern portion (e.g. Geus 2018; Roller 2010: 30–7).

Describing the surrounding world could be done at various scales and in various ways, using different tools and methods, depending on the final aims. In the II century CE, Claudios Ptolemaios, the Greek astronomer based in Alexandria, made a distinction between regional and world cartography, respectively called *chorographia* (literally 'description of a country') and *geographia*:

> The goal of regional cartography is an impression of a part, as when one makes an image of just an ear or an eye; but the goal of world cartography is a general view, analogous to making a portrait of the whole head. That is, whenever a portrait is to be made, one has to fit in the main parts of the body in a determined pattern and an order of priority. (…) Regional cartography deals above all with the qualities rather than the quantities of the things that it sets down (…). World cartography, on the other hand, deals with the quantities more than the qualities (…). For these reasons, regional cartography has no need of mathematical method, but here, in world cartography, this element takes absolute precedence'.
>
> (Ptol. *Geog.* 1.2, 4 and 5)

The picture was completed by *topographia*, the description of the specific characteristics of a place (Curry 2005). *Chorographia* also appears to concern the level of the place, whereas *geographia* might be paired to the realm of space: the former corresponds to a self-contained combination of elements that can be experienced together (from the ground), while the latter to a schematic, potentially unlimited pattern to be applied (from the air, in literal or metaphorical terms) to measure the world that surrounds us.

Mathematical data and geometrical calculations played a fundamental role in the progressive systematisation of the information on shape, dimensions, and distribution of the known territories (cf. Agnew and Livingstone 2011: 24–5). Travelling, however, did not necessarily rely on this type of data: moving on land and water heavily depended on objective factors such as the presence (or the absence) of roads and bridges and on the weather conditions that travellers would encounter during their journeys, as well as on the subjective, physical abilities of the travellers themselves. Travellers and sailors therefore relied on a different, intuitive, more practical geographical knowledge, which was based on commonsensical experience and not necessarily on scientific understanding, that in many cases would presumably be of little practical assistance (Geus and Thiering 2012: 2 and 4; see also Holt-Jensen 2018: 4–5 and Dan et al. 2016).

These two aspects of geographical knowledge, geometrical (the bird's-eye view, and its technologically updated version, the satellite view) and commonsensical (the evergreen ground-level experience) worked in parallel and, at the same time, overlapped at interlocking scales: travelling concerned a larger number of individuals in comparison with the number of theorists who studied shape and dimensions of the Earth; and yet information on distant lands spread thanks to the work of a relatively small number of scholars. The knowledge of the surrounding world derived from a combination of all these elements, and the 'description of the Earth' developed and evolved as both travels and calculations progressively pushed beyond their limits.

Here, there, and everywhere

Travelling brought the Greeks in contact with territories that differed from their own in terms of shape and environment. Eratosthenes divided the Earth into five zones: two polar, two temperate, and one equatorial in the middle. A similar division can be already found in the *Meteorologika* ('Meteorology') of Aristoteles (Arist., *Mete*. 2.5), written in the mid-IV century BCE, and may date back to the slightly earlier work of Eudoxus of Cnidos, who suggested that the world 'sloped' to the north and south poles (Roller 2010: 144). The Greek word for 'slope' is *klima*, from which originate the modern words meaning 'climate' in the majority of European languages.

Mediterranean populations perceived the local climate as ideal. Herodotos wrote that the 'Ionians (…), of all men whom we know, happened to found their cities in places with the loveliest of climate and seasons' (Hdt. 1.142.1). Five centuries later, the Greek geographer Strabo listed the reasons for Italy's prosperity: its insular position, the quality of its harbours, and the ideal climate to sustain the life of animals and plants (Str. 6.4.1). In the same period, the Roman architect Vitruvius noted that 'it seems necessary to develop the types of building in one way in Egypt, another way in Hispania, still differently in Pontus, otherwise in Rome, and so on, according to the distinctive properties of other lands and regions' (Vitr. *De arch.* 6.1.1).

The perception that the environment shaped also bodies and minds lay at the foundation of the Greek treatise better known by its Latin title *De aere, aquis et locis* ('Airs, waters and places'), belonging to the corpus of works attributed to the Greek physician Hippocrates, a contemporary of Herodotos, who is conventionally labelled as the 'Father of Medicine' (Futo Kennedy 2016: 19–22; Thomas 2000: chapter 3). The first paragraph explains that, in order to investigate medicine, one must take into account the seasons, the winds, the water, and the orientation and exposure to the sun of populations and settlements. As a consequence, the author stated that the mild and constant weather enjoyed by Asian populations prevented them from developing 'courage, endurance of suffering, laborious enterprise, and high spirit' (Hippoc. *Aer* 16; cf. Hansen 2000: 143), and that, instead, the people dwelling 'on the northern borders of Europe and Asia (…) experience regular shocks (…) as the weather and landscape change, thus making them courageous, antisocial and passionate' (Hippoc. *Aer* 23.4, Futo Kennedy 2016: 20). Vitruvius later followed the same line, by noting that

> the southern nations, having minds sharp with heat, move more quickly and efficiently to the inventions of ideas: the northern populations, infused with the thickness of the air and chilled by moisture, have sluggish minds because of this air's resistance.
>
> (Vitr. *De arch.* 6.1.9)

Nowadays, any official statement along these lines would cause an international diplomatic brawl. And yet these concepts periodically resurface in the most common stereotypes, especially in times of crisis. They are brilliantly visualised in the sarcastic *Atlas of Prejudices*, an ongoing project available both in print and on the web, collecting maps of the world (or of parts of it) 'according to' various points of view, mostly politically incorrect (Tsvetko 2017). Differences are, and have always been, a powerful tool to establish identities (Gruen 2011; also Skinner 2012), but the step that follows this apparently neutral consideration is a slippery one, as there is a dangerously thin line dividing the differentiation of places and people from what we now call racism.

Looking back at the past from our privileged satellite point of view, *De aere, aquis et locis* can be considered as the origin of environmental determinism, which has seen periods of alternating fortune, including a peak between the XVIII and the XIX centuries (Futo Kennedy and Jones-Lewis 2016; Livingstone 2012: 581–2; Painter and Jeffrey 2009: 177–9; Wear 2008; Cary 1949; Febvre 1925; George 1901 just to mention some). In the most extreme cases, the role of the environment in the development of a population was considered to be totally predominant. Determinism, both in its neo-Lamarckian version and under the broad label of social Darwinism, backed the growth and implementation of imperialism. It is not a coincidence that the development of the geographical societies that flourished in the XIX century and promoted the exploration of foreign lands is deeply intertwined with that of colonialism (Holt-Jensen 2018: chapter 3).

The conquest of those who are, in turn, perceived as naturally inferior populations has been a constant of history; if events that took place in a distant past have been investigated in detail, we are however still far from a full elaboration of the relatively recent European colonial past (Futo Kennedy 2016; Gregory et al. 2009: 196–7; Howe 2002, just to mention a few). A specific aspect of this broader issue, which is the focus of a series of recent studies, is the legitimacy of some Western museums to retain objects removed from their original contexts in colonial times, on the occasions of blatantly violent acts, as well as in breach or in absence of laws preventing their removal (e.g. Hicks 2020 and Robertson 2019, respectively).

Against determinism, the XIX century saw the development of a possibilistic approach, which focused on the futility of drawing boundaries between natural and cultural phenomena and triggered a wave of regional studies (see Holt-Jensen 2018: 115). The relationship between space and place has been the subject of a long debate (Agnew 2011), in which the phenomenological approach, spanning from Aristoteles to Heidegger, inspired Shapin (1998: 6) to write that there is no 'view from nowhere' and that knowledge is always 'local, situated, and embedded', and Casey (1996: 18) to conclude that 'to live is to live locally, and to know is, first of all, to know the places one is in'.

Archaeological studies also incorporated this debate. In 1970 Vita-Finzi and Higgs introduced the concept of 'site catchment analysis', that is, the study of the basin from which a settlement derived its resources, to be measured in walking time rather than bare distances, as the local topography might impede some movements (Vita-Finzi and Higgs 1970; for a short summary, see Bailey 2005: 172–6). This approach led to the development of a wave of studies dedicated to the influence of the major climate changes in the Mediterranean environment on the evolution of ancient societies (Broodbank 2013: 80–1; Horden and Purcell 2000: 318; Vita-Finzi 1969).

12 *Limits*

In general, it is now an established fact that the study of the past is deeply intertwined with the study of the environment. Landscape archaeology sets specific monuments within their wider territorial frame, using a combination of traditional and new technological instruments and solutions (Bintliff 2019; Jones 2005; Anschuetz, Wilshusen, and Scheick 2001; Ucko and Leyton 1999; Aston 1985), and is able to reconstruct the various uses of an area over time (Johnson 2005); of course, the interpretation of the raw data is crucial to obtain reliable results (see for instance Hodder 2012a: 11–27 for the use of analogy in archaeology). More specifically, the role of phenomenology in archaeology has been a matter of a heated debate centred on the need to find a balance between physically experiencing a landscape and using abstract tools to analyse it (e.g. Brück 2005 and Johnson 2012 on the discussion triggered by Tilley 1994 and 2004). If we pair these two approaches, respectively, to the ground-level and the satellite view, we may conclude that they are both necessary to grasp the big picture (cf. Langton 1988: 21).

Mapping the journey

The word 'culture' comes from the Latin verb *colĕre*, to cultivate, and means more or less 'produce'. As such, it conveys a sedentary flavour that certainly reflected the life of a large number of ancient people, busy as they were producing the food that they needed to survive. Apart from living in one place and moving around in the same area, some people entrusted with specific tasks also travelled, that is, went from place to place (cf. Casey 1996: 23–4). Travelling allowed to transport people, goods, and information, and represented a pillar of trade and warfare. If the Greeks expanded their radius of action along the Mediterranean coasts mainly to increase their trading activities, the Romans created the most efficient communication network of the ancient world mainly to militarily control their large territory (Dueck 2012: 10–9, also 111–2).

The evolution of modern geography proceeded in parallel with the exploration of the Earth, and with the development of cartography (Harley 1987), but in ancient times maps did not have a pivotal function (Curry 2005). Their use in ancient Greece and Rome, for instance, is a matter of debate (Adams and Laurence 2001). We possess direct and indirect evidence of the existence of several representations of portions of the known world dating to Antiquity, either as physical fragments or through written descriptions (Dilke 1985, 1987). Different words were used to indicate different types of maps: in Latin, *forma* was used to indicate the shape of a territory, *descriptio* for a world map; *mappa* (lit. 'cloth'), *charta* (lit. 'papyrus'), and *tabula* (lit. 'board', equivalent to the Greek *pinax*) referred instead to the physical substance of the various documents (Dilke 1985: appendix VI). Each of these types of maps presented a selection of data, chosen by the map-maker and picked up by the map-reader, presumably thanks to graphic conventions that tried to reduce the gap due to subjective interpretations (cf. Clarke 1999: 25–6; see also Malpas 2018: chapter 2).

A specific discussion concerns the issue of the existence of scale maps. Brodersen (2001) argued that the Romans did not have them, as they did not need them: the organisation of the information into *itineraria* (itineraries), which listed distances between rest-stations, contained and conveyed all that a traveller could need. Travelling across the Roman Empire was an eminently practical issue, and was supported by eminently practical, informative documents.

If itineraries sufficed to travel (including trade and military operations), the branch of geography concerning the theoretical calculations on the extent of the known world and precise position of cities and geographical features continued to develop, and reached its apex in the II century CE thanks to the work of Claudios Ptolemaios and his main source, Marinus of Tyros. He experimented with three different projections of the round Earth on a flat surface, but none of them proved satisfactory for a detailed, comprehensive map; he therefore recommended the first method to draw the general map, and the use of orthogonal grids to draw regional maps to an acceptable approximation (Dilke 1985: 78–80).

His text was clearly associated with a number of maps, which he explicitly listed; however, it is unclear whether these maps were actually contained in his original manuscript. Our knowledge of the text depends on about fifty copies, the earliest of which date to the end of the XIII century; some of them contain large maps, but it is unlikely that they were direct copies of now-lost originals, as at the time of Claudios Ptolemaios not even the tallest papyrus roll would have been able to accommodate a detailed world map. It is possible that the maps did not actually accompany the text but were displayed in a public space, as happened in Rome with Agrippa's map in the I century CE, and at Augustodunum two centuries later (Berggren and Jones 2000: 45–50).

Nowadays, we extensively use maps to illustrate and to communicate information; I myself use them in this book. We may also use them to 'reconstruct' the ancient world, by combining modern shapes and ancient texts (e.g. Morkot 1996: 82 and Dilke 1985). These representations may be extremely useful, among us, as they are able to convey some basic concepts in a quick and direct way; they clearly show, for instance, not only the shape of the known world as geographical knowledge evolved, but also the growing extent of the known lands that were progressively incorporated into these maps. It is important to underline, however, that these representations are schematic depictions of the ancient sources. The reader should be careful and treat them as 'translations' into another 'language', and not as primary sources, as they introduce a number of modern elements and criteria into the scene (such as north at the top, the shape of the coasts, etc.) that may be misleading (cf. Brodersen's scepticism in Dueck 2012: 101).

At any rate, if we look at the general history of cartography, we can see how new portions of Earth progressively appeared on the world's representations, proceeding in parallel with travels and explorations. Some of these areas were uninhabited, whereas others were inhabited but had never been mapped in a scientific way within the world's larger frame. Of course, cartography does not necessarily certify the advent of humans in a certain area, but only the advent of a cartographer.

By the first half of the XX century, only a few blank areas remained to be filled; one of these was the Sahara, the largest hot desert in the world, stretching for over nine million square kilometres, and representing a good example on which to discuss the scope of this book.

The history of the modern exploration of its Egyptian portion, called the Western or Libyan Desert, is deeply related to the development of motorised vehicles. From the World War I Light Car Patrols captained by General Archibald Murray, to the World War II Long Range Desert Group established by the experienced explorer Ralph Bagnold, desert explorers tested, on sand, Model T Fords, Rolls Royce armoured cars, Citroën half-tracks, and eventually Model A Fords (Goudie 2008). Particularly meaningful is the story of one of the most famous desert explorers, László Almásy (Bierman 2004). In 1926, while working as representative of the Austrian car firm Steyr, he drove one of their cars along the Nile into Sudan, an enterprise never carried out before with an ordinary car. This trip represented a turning point in his life: in the subsequent ten years he carried out several expeditions into the Libyan Desert by car, during which he discovered and mapped geographical features as well as important prehistoric sites (Almásy 1939).

The advent of cars, railway and planes changed trade and travel along the Nile in the space of one generation (Almásy 1939: chapter 1). Despite the fact that cars were faster and required less resources in comparison with camels and their attendants, not all explorers appreciated this change (Goudie 2008: 46–7). The introduction of motorised vehicles probably contributed to sealing the fate of a number of small water stations in the desert stretching between Egypt and Sudan. As cars progressively took over pack animals, the maintenance of small water sources became inconstant, if not unnecessary, and eventually the wind-blown sand suffocated them.

The introduction of cars offered (apparently) unlimited chances to discover and explore new areas, but one must not forget that these vehicles, too, have their own limitations: cars travel along certain paths, whereas people, camels, and donkeys may travel along others. In 1999 the German explorer Carlo Bergmann led a caravan of camels from the Oasis of Dakhla towards the Gilf al-Kebir: he and his camels did not proceed along the well-beaten car-track used by motorised tourists and desert travellers heading to the Gilf, and along *their* way he discovered a previously unknown line of ancient Egyptian water stations that had been set up and used by ancient caravans of donkeys (Förster 2015). Until then, only one such water stations was known, Abu Ballas, which evidently corresponded to the intersection between the two routes running along different lines, the most convenient for camels and the most convenient for cars. This revealing episode confirms once more the necessity to carefully evaluate how modern travel methods may shape our understanding of the past.

Connections

Realms

Boundaries, conventional or physical, are instrumental to defining what is included within; they are also voluntarily or involuntarily porous to various degrees (Casey 1996: 42). The systematisation of our knowledge follows similar, unwritten rules.

'Ancient' Egypt, Greece, and Rome conventionally correspond to precise periods of the long history of these three civilisations: ancient Egypt covers over thirty centuries, ancient Greece about twenty, and Rome about twelve. This ancient world ended, in a way, with the fall of the Roman Empire, which had included them all under the same umbrella. If plotted along a timeline, these three civilisations span most of human history (Figure 1.1): ancient Egypt, by itself, covers twice the time that separates us from the fall of the Roman Empire. As we shall see, over this extremely long period, Egypt's territorial extent remained basically stable; in contrast, the staggering rise and growth of Rome's area of influence took place within only 500 years, between the IV century BCE and the I century CE.

The ancient Egyptian state was born along the Nile around 3000 BCE, together with a first version of the hieroglyphic writing system, and therefore with history in its conventional sense. Egypt enjoyed twenty centuries of relatively undisturbed power and independence, then ten more centuries of less stable conditions, and eventually lost its independence to Rome in the year 30 BCE. In a completely different scenario, Greek civilisation owes its origins and development to movements and migrations that took place across the Aegean and Ionian Seas, and the territories around them, even before the beginning of the Bronze Age (c. 3300 BCE). By the VIII century BCE, city-states started to gain prominence in mainland, peninsular, and

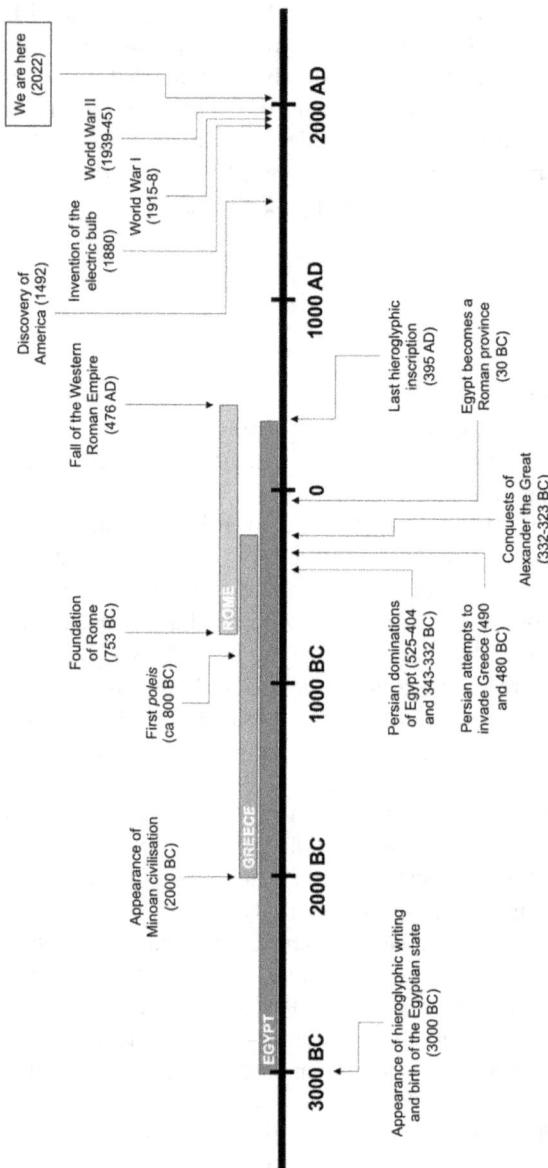

Figure 1.1 Timeline.

insular Greece and gave birth to a lively trade network that progressively spanned the Mediterranean (cf. Osborne 2009).

In the IV century BCE, Alexander the Great briefly absorbed this galaxy of interdependent and interconnected entities into one 'empire', spanning all the way to Egypt, Mesopotamia, and beyond. After his unexpected death, this large territory was divided into large chunks, assigned to his most important generals. The circulation of goods and information across the Mediterranean (and beyond) characterised the so-called Hellenistic period, which conventionally terminates with the rise of Roman superpower. Born as a small, nondescript village along the River Tiber in the VIII century BCE, Rome managed to create the largest ancient empire by the beginning of the II century CE, and to maintain it until the end of the V century CE in the west, and one more century in the east. Unlike Egypt and Greece, Rome expanded over a vast area consisting of a variety of territories and cultures, characterised by completely different environmental conditions.

Of course Egyptians, Greeks, and Romans were not alone, as they shared ancient stage, over the centuries, with a number of other actors (Horden and Purcell 2000): these included both centralised states, such as the ones that developed in Mesopotamia, and populations belonging to groups or networks, such as the ones labelled as 'Phoenicians' (e.g. Quinn 2017) and 'Germanic peoples' (e.g. Burns 2003; Wells 1999). Discussing them all, not to mention their interactions, is out of the scope of this book. The choice of focusing on Egypt, Greece, and Rome depends on two interconnected factors, both subjective to different degrees.

The first is the significant link that these three civilisations acknowledged among themselves, and that we still perceive nowadays. In some instances, they are so deeply interconnected to be indissolubly entangled (e.g. Spier, Potts, and Cole 2018; Rutherford 2016; Bagnall 1993). The Greeks looked at Egypt with awe and reverence:

> you Greeks are always children. (...) You are young in soul, every one of you. For therein you possess not a single belief that is ancient and derived from old tradition, nor yet one science that is hoary with age.

This is supposed to have been said by an Egyptian priest to a Greek visitor (Pl., *Tim.* 22; cf. Assmann 2011: xi). Concerning Rome's interaction with Greece, as Horatius put it, *Graecia capta ferum victorem cepit et artes intulit agresti Latio* ('conquered Greece conquered the savage conqueror and brought arts into rustic Latium', Hor. *Epist.* 2.1, 156–7).

The second is the deep link that the sociocultural group to which I belong (southern European scholars) acknowledges with the Graeco-Roman culture, and therefore also with Egypt. Born and raised in cities founded by either the Greeks or the Romans, the Graeco-Roman culture constitutes a substantial part first of our *curriculum vitae*, then also of our *curriculum studiorum*. This boils down to the rather prosaic fact that I am familiar with these three languages, and can directly deal with the original sources.

The tendency to always refer back to the *ensemble* Egypt-Greece-Rome might be taken as a simplification of past events. Simplifying, however, must not be necessarily taken in its negative sense: in the introduction of his book on the history of geography, Holt-Jensen (2018: xvi) notes that 'every scientific presentation is a simplification'. On the other hand, our identity is also shaped by our individual perception of ourselves. In this respect, the present study certainly moves within a very specific circle, with all its limitations. However, in my intention, stating these limitations simply helps to identify the path along which this particularly study has been carried out, without implying that no other study is possible or valid. It will simply need another scholar to be carried out.

Scales

As mentioned above, this book focuses on the relationship between the description of the Earth at ground level and that from the air, on how the commonsensical and compartmentalised experience of travellers contributed to building an overall picture of the known world, and on how experiencing places determined the construction of mental spaces.

The dichotomies *chorographia/geographia*, commonsensical and geometric approach, ground-level and satellite views, place and space are clear if seen from the distance: they offer a useful method to distinguish between practical actions and theoretical abstraction. The closer one gets to the details, however, the less clear this distinction appears.

What distinguishes these realms of action is the scale, ranging from the field of view of the traveller on his donkey or the sailor on his boat, to the Earth's projections of Claudios Ptolemaios. Travellers needed measures to make plans and keep track of their progression through time and an uninterrupted flow of places. Geographers needed measures to construct an abstract spatial cage into which they could fit the Earth, ignoring the singularity and individuality of places. The common element is thus represented by the act of measuring, which would be performed at different scales and in different ways, depending on its specific purpose.

In the end, what divides the two realms is not a precise line, but a grey area, which is probably the best representation of the reality. People generally use a varying combination of tools (mental and practical) to achieve their needs. These tools, in turn, are not always exactly the same as they may depend on differing combinations of different needs.

The codification of space, the most abstract form of *geo-graphia*, eventually depends on the progressive appropriation of a sequence of places. Therefore, Claudios Ptolemaios, and the traveller or the sailor just looked at the same world from two different points of view. The donkey and the boat, the route and the waves, were not secondary elements, as they determined if and how knowledge could be gained, and then transmitted, stored, and elaborated in texts and drawings.

Humans, things, and places

As Geertz simply noted, 'no one lives in the world in general' (1996: 262). And this applies both to the present and to the past.

The ancient Egyptian civilisation developed along the Nile Valley. Its history is inextricably bound to its territory, and to the peculiar environmental conditions: the annual inundation dictated rhythms and rules that applied to the entire population, and shaped their daily life and religious beliefs. Ancient Egypt has been rarely mentioned in this first chapter as the Egyptians do not appear to have taken a 'geo-graphical' interest in the world in the way the Greeks did. As we shall see below, however, even if not codified in writing, the 'description of their Earth' imbued nearly every ancient Egyptian artistic and architectural enterprise that has come down to us. Virtually every aspect of their view of life and death is emplaced and rooted in the local environment and landscape.

The Egyptians were accomplished sailors throughout their entire history. Most of their transports and movements took place along the Nile; in comparison to the river, the sea, called 'the Great Green', represented a less familiar environment. Nevertheless, from time to time, long-range maritime expeditions to reach distant lands for commercial reasons took place both in the Mediterranean and in the Red Sea. The Egyptians also travelled overland, across the two deserts that bordered the Nile Valley. In particular, the oases of the Western Desert represented convenient bases for long-range commercial desert expeditions into deep Africa. All these movements, which varied in intensity and radius depending on the historical periods, remained always centred on the Nile Valley.

The ancient Greek civilisation, instead, was born out of intensive commercial exchanges across the maze of islands and jagged coasts of the Aegean Sea. Seafaring represented a founding pillar of its entire history; travelling on land was less convenient, and was restricted to inevitable occasions. The Greeks expanded their trade routes along the Mediterranean coasts by replicating always the same scheme consisting of a network of interdependent entities.

Rome, or – to be precise – the Roman Empire, managed to piece together a huge area consisting of land and water. The land included completely different territories, ranging from damp and cold Britain to hot and dry Libya, from the German woods to the Syrian desert, from the granaries of Spain to those of Egypt. Waters under Roman control included major rivers (fully incorporated into the empire, such as the Nile and the Po, as well as waterlines acting as boundaries, such as the Rhine and Danube) and the vast expanse of the entire Mediterranean Sea, which took the name of *Mare Nostrum* ('Our Sea'). The role of the Mediterranean Sea in shaping the development of the civilisations that lived around its shores has recently been the subject of intense research and debate (Broodbank 2013; Horden and Purcell 2000). Modern studies have also analysed in detail the history of travels (Casson 1994), and highlighted how in the Roman period the 'Middle Sea' was criss-crossed by trading and military expeditions, often in continuity with land itineraries (Adams and Laurence 2001).

Human aggregation can take different forms depending on the surrounding environment, which also shapes the external relations of the aggregated group. These, in turn, depend on travelling, encompassing the transport of people, goods, and information, and travelling takes place across the surrounding environment, that therefore acts both as a defining and as a connective element. The way in which we look at, perceive, and describe the world that surrounds us is deeply related to our cultural identity and influences our decisions. In this respect, geography shapes history.

Cornford (1912: 54) wrote that behind philosophy lay religion, and behind religion lay social custom, the structure and institutions of the human group. I would add that the latter are in turn shaped by the territory where the human group lives, in two ways: as a physical scenario into which everything is rooted (perceived and described: the *geo-graphia*), and as the possibility to establish communication lines (how people travelled). The physical environment plays an active role in the construction of the connective structure of each culture, made of memory, identity, and cultural continuity (cf. Assmann 2011: 2). After all, Hodder's entanglement between humans and things (humans depend on things, things depend on other things and things depend on humans, Hodder 2012b) literally 'takes place' in a precise environment and along specific physical connections, and place is where space and time come together (Casey 1996: 36). To close the circle: 'just as personal memory and identity is tied directly to place and locality, so too are cultural "memory" and identity tied to landscape and the physical environment' (Malpas 2018: 190, Figure 1.2).

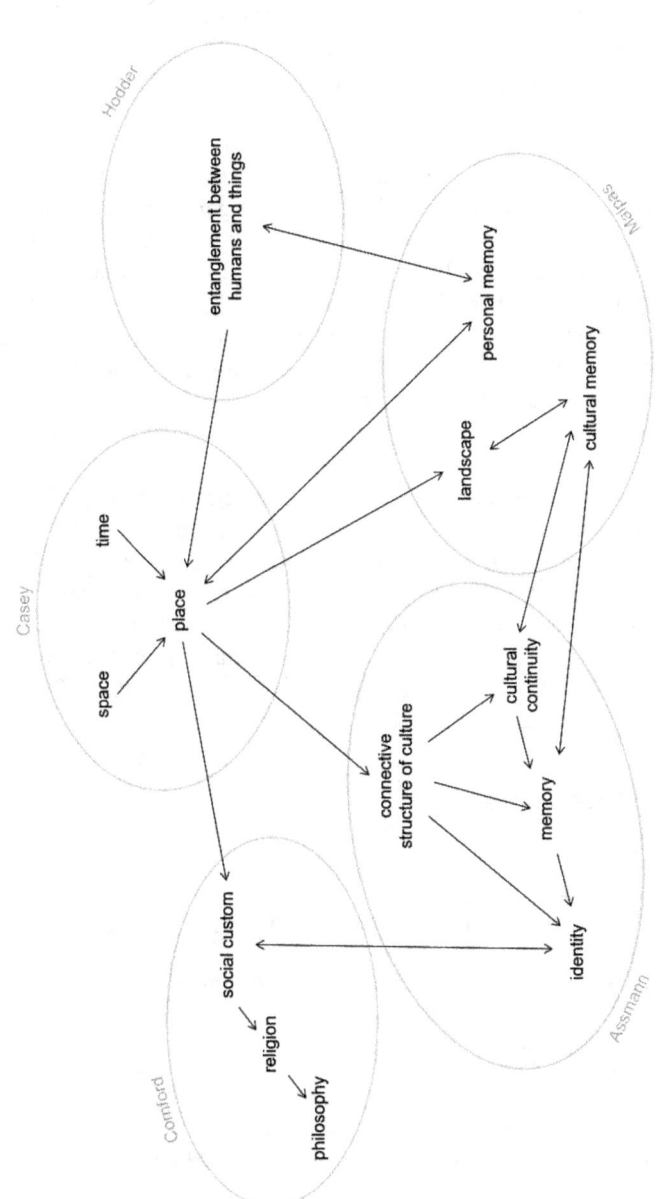

Figure 1.2 Concept map.

If a first step to improve our understanding of *what* happened in the distant past (the historical element) can be reached by considering *where* it happened (the traditional geographical element), a further level of improvement can be achieved by taking into account together *where* and *how* things happened, as these two aspects are strictly related and interdependent. Setting a historical event in a geographical area helps, but *placing* it in relation to a specific context may offer the chance to further refine our understanding. As Malpas summarised:

> Just as the narratives that structure subjectivity are directly tied to action and movement, so too are the narratives that belong to places and landscapes (to which the narratives that are internalised in subjectivity are connected) tied to the possibilities that are inherent in those places and landscapes, and that are part of their very fabric. (…) The landscape in which we find ourselves, and through which we are defined, is thus as much a part of what we are – of our minds, our actions, and our serves – as is the food we eat and the air we breathe.
>
> (Malpas 2018: 190–1)

The following chapters contain a brief description of how the Egyptian, Greek, and Roman civilisations experienced, perceived, and described their worlds, where they lived, evolved, and created their cultural memory. The Ariadne's thread that will guide this attempt across the vast labyrinth of knowledge accumulated on these three cultures will be an analysis of how people moved within their place and from place to place. Movement is a primary condition to achieve an appropriation and a codification of the space, that in turn shapes choices and decisions.

Bibliographical references

Primary sources

Arist. *Mete.*: Aristoteles, *Meteorologica*.
Hdt.: Herodotus, *Historiae*. English translation from the Perseus Digital Library (perseus.tufts.edu).
Hippoc. *Aer.*: Hippocrates, *De aere, aquis et locis*. English translation from The Internet Classic Archive (classics.mit.edu).
Hor. *Epist.*: Horatius, *Epistolae*.
Pl. *Tim.*: Plato, *Timaeus*. English translation from the Perseus Digital Library (perseus.tufts.edu).
Ptol. *Geog.*: Ptolemaeus, *Geographia*. English translation from Berggren J. L. and Jones A. 2000. *Ptolemy's Geography*. Princeton/Oxford, Princeton University Press.

Str.: Strabo, *Geographia*.English translation from the Perseus Digital Library (perseus.tufts.edu).
Vitr. *De arch.*: Vitruvius, *De architectura*. English translation from Rowland I. D. and Howe T. Noble. 1999. *Vitruvius. Ten Books on Architecture*. Cambridge, Cambridge University Press.

Secondary sources

Adams C. and Laurence R. (eds.) 2001. *Travel and Geography in the Roman Empire*. London/New York, Routledge.
Agnew J. A. 2011. 'Space and Place', in J. A. Agnew and D. N. Livingstone (eds.), *The SAGE Handbook of Geographical Knowledge*. London, SAGE: 316–30.
Agnew J. A. and Livingstone D. N. (eds.) 2011. *The SAGE Handbook of Geographical Knowledge*. London, SAGE.
Almásy L. 1939. *Unbekannte Sahara*. Leipzig, Brockhaus.
Anschuetz K. F., Wilshusen R. H. and Scheick C. L. 2001. 'An Archaeology of Landscapes: Perspectives and Directions', *Journal of Archaeological Research* 9.2: 157–211.
Assmann J. 2011. *Cultural Memory and Early Civilization: Writing, Remembrance, and Political Imagination*. Cambridge, Cambridge University Press.
Aston M. 1985. *Interpreting the Landscape: Landscape Archaeology and Local History*. London/New York, Routledge.
Bagnall R. 1993. *Egypt in Late Antiquity*. Princeton, Princeton University Press.
Bailey G. 2005. 'Site Catchment Analysis', in C. Renfrew and P. Bahn (eds.), *Archaeology, The Key Concepts*. London/New York, Routledge: 172–6.
Baker A. R. H. 2003. *Geography and History: Bridging the Divide*. Cambridge, Cambridge University Press.
Berggren J. L. and Jones A. 2000. *Ptolemy's Geography*. Princeton/Oxford, Princeton University Press.
Bierman J. 2004. *The Secret Life of Laszlo Almasy*. London, Penguin.
Bintliff J. L. 2019. 'Postface. Mapping Historical Landscapes in Transition: An Overview', in T. Coomans, B. Cattoor and K. De Jonge (eds.), *Mapping Landscapes in Transformation Multidisciplinary Methods for Historical Analysis*. Leuven, Leuven University Press: 349–66.
Brodersen K. 2001. 'The Presentation of the Geographical Knowledge for Travel and Transportation in the Roman world', in C. Adams and R. Laurence (eds.), *Travel and Geography in the Roman Empire*. London/New York, Routledge: 7–21.
Broodbank C. 2013. *The Making of the Middle Sea: A History of the Mediterranean from the Beginning to the Emergence of the Classical World*. London, Thames and Hudson.
Brück J. 2005. 'Experiencing the Past? The Development of a Phenomenological Archaeology in British Prehistory', *Archaeological Dialogues* 12.1: 45–72.
Burns T. S. 2003. *Rome and the Barbarians, 100 B.C.–A.D. 400*. Baltimore, Johns Hopkins University Press.

Cary M. 1949. *The Geographical Background of Greek and Roman History*. Oxford, Clarendon Press.
Casey E. S. 1996. 'How to Get from Space to Place in a Fairly Short Stretch of Time', in S. Feld and K. H. Basso (eds.), *Senses of Place*. Santa Fe, School for Advanced Research Press: 13–52.
Casson L. 1994. *Travel in the Ancient World*. Baltimore/London, Johns Hopkins University Press.
Clarke K. 1999. *Between Geography and History: Hellenistic Constructions of the Roman World*. Oxford Classical Monographs. Oxford, Clarendon Press.
Cornford F. M. 1912. *From Religion to Philosophy: A Study in the Origins of Western Speculation* (1991 edition). Princeton, Princeton University Press.
Curry M. R. 2005. 'Toward a Geography of a World without Maps: Lessons from Ptolemy and Postal Codes', *Annals of the Association of American Geographers* 95.3: 680–91.
Dan A., Crom W., Geus K., Görz G., Guckelsberger K., König V., Poiss T. and Thiering M. 2016. 'Common Sense Geography and Ancient Geographical Texts', *Journal for Ancient Studies*, Special Volume 6 - Space and Knowledge: 571–97.
Darby H. C. 1953. 'On the Relations of Geography and History', *Transactions and Papers (Institute of British Geographers)* 19: 1–11.
Dilke O. A. W. 1985. *Greek and Roman Maps*. London, Thames and Hudson.
Dilke O. A. W. 1987. 'Cartography in the Ancient World: A Conclusion', in J. B. Harley and D. Woodward (eds.), *History of Cartography*, vol. 1. Chicago, University of Chicago Press, chapter 16: 276–9.
Dueck D. 2012. *Geography in Classical Antiquity*. Cambridge, Cambridge University Press.
Febvre L. 1925. *A Geographical Introduction to History*. Translated by E. G. Mountford and J. H. Paxton. London, Kegan Paul/Trench/Trubner and Co.
Förster F. 2015. *Der Abu Ballas-Weg: Eine pharaonische Karawanenroute durch die Libysche Wüste*, Africa Praehistorica 28. Köln, Heinrich-Barth-Institut.
Futo Kennedy R. 2016. 'Airs, Waters, Metals, Earth: People and Environment in Archaic and Classical Greek Thought', in R. Futo Kennedy and M. Jones-Lewis (eds.), *The Routledge Handbook of Identity and the Environment in the Classical and Medieval Worlds*. London, Routledge: 9–28.
Futo Kennedy R. and Jones-Lewis M. 2016. *The Routledge Handbook of Identity and the Environment in the Classical and Medieval Worlds*. London, Routledge.
Geertz C. 1996. 'Afterword', in S. Feld and K. H. Basso (eds.), *Senses of Place*. Santa Fe, School for Advanced Research Press: 259–62.
George H. B. 1901. *The Relations of Geography & History*. Oxford, Clarendon Press.
Geus K. 2018. 'Greek and Greco-Roman Geography', in A. Jones and L. Taub (eds.), *The Cambridge History of Science. Vol. 1: Ancient Science*. Cambridge, Cambridge University Press: 402–12.
Geus K and Thiering M. 2012. 'Common Sense Geography and Mental Modelling: Setting the Stage', in K. Geus and M. Thiering (eds.), *Common Sense Geography and Mental Modelling*. Berlin, Max Planck Institute for the History of Science, MPIWG Preprint 426: 2–10.

Goudie A. 2008. *Wheels across the Desert: Exploration of the Libyan Desert by Motocar 1916–1942*. London, Silphium.
Gregory D., Johnston R., Pratt G., Watts M. and Whatmore S. 2009. *The Dictionary of Human Geography* (5th edition). Hoboken, Wiley.
Gruen E. S. 2011. *Rethinking the Other in Antiquity*. Princeton/Oxford, Princeton University Press.
Hansen M. H. 2000. 'The Hellenic Polis', in H. H. Hansen (ed.), *A Comparative Study of Thirty City-State Cultures: An Investigation Conducted by the CPC*. Copenhagen, Reitzels Vorlag: 141–87.
Harley J. B. 1987. 'The Map and the Development of the History of Cartography', in J. B. Harley and D. Woodward (eds.), *History of Cartography*, vol. 1. Chicago, University of Chicago Press, chapter 1: 1–42.
Hartog F. 1988. *The Mirror of Herodotus: The Representation of the Other in the Writing of History*. Berkeley/Los Angeles/London, University of California Press.
Hicks D. 2020. *The Brutish Museum: The Benin Bronzes, Colonial Violence and Cultural Restitution*. London, Pluto Press.
Hodder I. 2012a. *The Present Past: An Introduction to Anthropology for Archaeologists*. Barnsley, Pen and Words Books.
Hodder I. 2012b. *Entangled: An Archaeology of the Relationships Between Humans and Things*. Oxford, John Wiley and Sons Inc.
Holt-Jensen A. 2018. *Geography: History and Concepts*. London/Los Angeles, SAGE.
Horden P. and Purcell N. 2000. *The Corrupting Sea: A Study of the Mediterranean History*. Malden/Oxford/Carlton, Blackwell Publishing.
Howe S. 2002. *Empire: A Very Short Introduction*. New York/Oxford, Oxford University Press.
Johnson M. H. 2005. 'Thinking about Landscape', in C. Renfrew and P. Bahn (eds.), *Archaeology, The Key Concepts*. London/New York, Routledge: 116–9.
Johnson M. H. 2012. 'Phenomenological Approaches in Landscape Archaeology', *Annual Review of Anthropology* 41: 269–84.
Jones M. 2005. 'Ecological Archaeology', in C. Renfrew and P. Bahn (eds.), *Archaeology, The Key Concepts*. London/New York, Routledge: 59–63.
Langton J. 1988. 'The Two Traditions of Geography, Historical Geography and the Study of Landscapes', *Geografiska Annaler* 70B: 17–25.
Livingstone D. N. 2012. 'Changing Climate, Human Evolution, and the Revival of Environmental Determinism', *Bulletin of the History of Medicine* 86.4: 564–95.
Malpas J. 2018. *Place and Experience: A Philosophical Topography* (2nd edition). London, Routledge.
Merrills A. H. 2005. *History and Geography in Late Antiquity*. Cambridge, Cambridge University Press.
Morkot R. 1996. *The Penguin Historical Atlas of Ancient Greece*. London, Penguin.
Osborne R. 2009. 'What Travelled with Greek Pottery?', in I. Malkin, C. Costantakopoulou and K. Panagopoulou (eds.), *Greek and Roman Networks in the Mediterranean*. London/New York, Routledge: 83–93.

Painter J. and Jeffrey A. 2009. *Political Geography: An Introduction to Space and Power* (2nd edition). London, SAGE.
Quinn J. 2017. *In Search of the Phoenicians*. Princeton, Princeton University Press.
Robertson G. 2019. *Who Owns History? Elgin's Loot and the Case for Returning Plundered Antiquities*. London, Biteback.
Roller D. W. 2010. *Eratosthenes' Geography*. Princeton/Oxford, Princeton University Press.
Rutherford I. (ed.) 2016. *Graeco-Egyptian Interactions: Literature, Translation, and Culture, 500 BC–AD 300*. Oxford, Oxford University Press.
Schepens G. 1980. *L''autopsie' dans la méthode des historiens grecs du Ve siècle avant J.-C*. Bruxelles, Palais des Académies.
Shapin S. 1998. 'Placing the View from Nowhere: Historical and Sociological Problems in the Location of Science', *Transactions of the Institute of British Geographers* 23.1: 5–12.
Skinner J. E. 2012. *The Invention of Greek Ethnography: From Homer to Herodotus*. Oxford, Oxford University Press.
Spier J., Potts T. and Cole S. E. (eds.) 2018. *Beyond the Nile: Egypt and the Classical World*. Los Angeles, Getty Publications.
Thomas R. 2000. *Herodotos in Context: Ethnography, Science and the Art of Persuasion*. Cambridge, Cambridge University Press.
Tilley C. 1994. *A Phenomenology of Landscape: Places, Paths and Monuments*. Oxford, Berg.
Tilley C. 2004. *The Materiality of Stone: Explorations in Landscape Phenomenology*. Oxford, Berg.
Tsvetko Y. 2017. *Atlas of Prejudice: The Complete Stereotype Map Collection*. London, Alphadesigner.
Ucko P. J. and Leyton R. (eds.) 1999. *The Archaeology and Anthropology of Landscape*. London/New York, Routledge.
Vita-Finzi C. 1969. *The Mediterranean Valleys*. Cambridge, Cambridge University Press.
Vita-Finzi C. and Higgs E. S. 1970. 'Prehistoric Economy in the Mount Carmel Area of Palestine: Site Catchment Analysis', *Proceedings of the Prehistoric Society* 36: 1–37.
Wear A. 2008. 'Place, Health, and Disease: The Airs, Waters, Places Tradition in Early Modern England and North America', *Journal of Medieval and Early Modern Studies* 38.3: 443–65.
Wells P. S. 1999. *The Barbarians Speak: How the Conquered Peoples Shaped Roman Europe*. Princeton and Oxford, Princeton University Press.

2 Ancient Egypt

> Hail to you, Ra, perfect each day, who rises at dawn without failing. (…) A moment is each day to you, it has passed when you go down. You also complete the hours of night, you order it without pause in your labor. Through you do all eyes see, they lack aim when your majesty sets. When you stir to rise at dawn, your brightness opens the eyes of the herds; when you set in the western mountain, they sleep in the state of death.
>
> (First hymn to the sun-god from the stele of Suti and Hor, 1–2, 18–27)

Places and cycles

Valley and deserts

A quick look at Egypt from Google Earth says it all: the green, narrow Valley snakes across the yellow surface of the desert northwards, and ends up in the green, wide Delta, from where the Nile discharges its waters into the Mediterranean Sea (Figure 2.1). This clear-cut distinction between Valley and Desert has been in existence since the desertification process turned the savannah that once stretched to the west into the present Sahara, about 6,000 years ago (e.g. Kuper 2002): since then, the presence of water has marked the limit of the habitable world or, in more dramatic terms, between life and death. If one travels out of the Valley, the green vegetation ceases abruptly at a certain distance from the river; from there onwards, there is only desert, until the next water source, which may pop up hundreds of kilometres away.

Throughout most of their history, the ancient Egyptians exercised full control on the Valley from the northern Delta to at least the First Cataract, as well as on a vast desert area, that included the Sinai, the entire Eastern Desert, and the chain of oases in the Western Desert (Figure 2.2). The First Cataract, in the area of modern Aswan, was the southernmost point that

28 *Ancient Egypt*

Figure 2.1 Physical map of Egypt, from Google Earth.

could be smoothly reached by boat and marked a convenient frontier for most of ancient Egyptian history. Nubia, the area between the First and the Fourth Cataract, was strongly influenced and periodically incorporated in the Egyptian state (O'Connor 1993; see van Pelt 2013 for a re-evaluation of the local social dynamics). Egyptian control of the Mediterranean coasts expanded in a significant way only briefly during the New Kingdom towards the east, and during the Ptolemaic period to the west (Figure 2.3).

Ancient Egypt 29

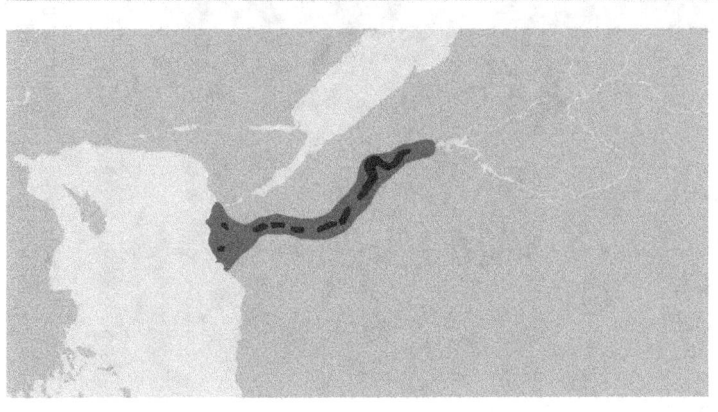

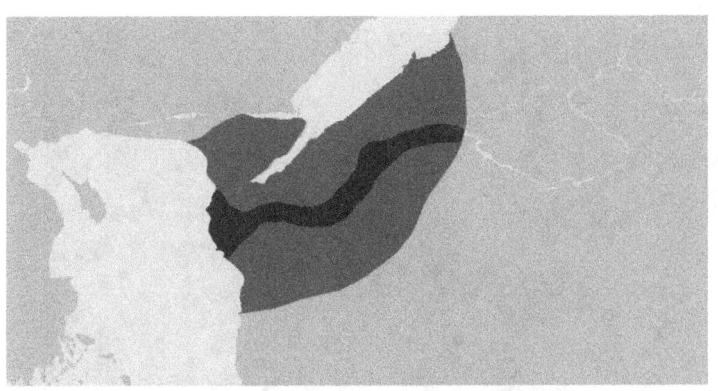

Figure 2.2 The territory of ancient Egypt (1): from left to right, the Valley and the territorial extent of the proto-states (3500–3000 BCE), of the Old Kingdom (2686–2181 BCE), and of the Middle Kingdom (2055–1650).

30 *Ancient Egypt*

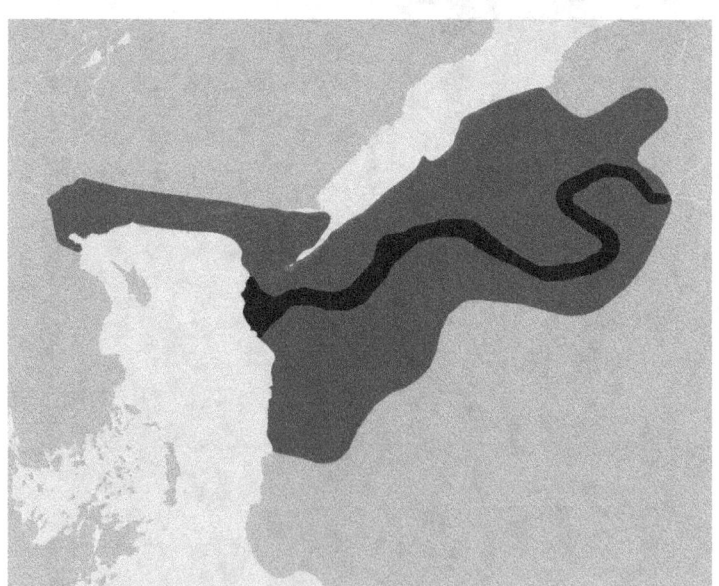

Figure 2.3 The territory of ancient Egypt (2): from left to right, the Valley and the territorial extent of the New Kingdom (1550–1077) and of the Ptolemaic period (305–30 BCE).

The River Nile has always represented the backbone of Egypt, the main communication route as well as the main source of water and food necessary to maintain the population. Even if most of the activities took place in and were centred on the Nile Valley, the territory that sustained and nourished the ancient Egyptian civilisation extended well beyond it. This was true in practical, as well as symbolic, terms. The deserts provided precious materials, metals, and stones: turquoise and copper from the Sinai; gold from the south-eastern desert; amethyst, alabaster and granite from the Eastern Desert; diorite and gneiss from the south-western desert; natron from the north-west (Aston, Harrell, and Shaw 2000; Ogden 2000). The deserts might act as buffer zones, but not necessarily as closed borders. Since the earliest periods, major caravan routes followed the chain of western and southern oases and took into Egypt and further north exotic products and materials from central Africa (e.g. Krzyszkowska and Morkot 2000). The deserts also played the role of defining the Valley, by physically bordering it and, at the same time, by representing its opposite.

The ancient Egyptian civilisation was deeply related to the particular environmental conditions of the Valley, to its spaces and annual rhythms. The Nile designed a surprisingly simple, symmetrical, and cyclical world: the river flowed from south to north; every day, the sun crossed the sky from east to west; every year the river covered most of the land for four months and changed the face of the habitable world. A large-scale, orderly mechanism appeared to regulate all aspects of life, including power, life, and death. This overall balance was called *ma'at* (Assmann 1990): it had divine origins, but was guaranteed by the ruling king, in a symmetrical mirror game that combined earth and sky, nature and power, life and death, ground-level perception and bird's-eye view.

Water and power

Every year, the constant flow of the White Nile, coming from the region of the Great Lakes of central Africa, was joined by the torrential discharge of the Blue Nile, fed by the seasonal rains on the Ethiopian mountains. Every year, in early June, the Nile would start rising in the area of Aswan; the water would proceed northwards and progressively cover most of the land, reaching a peak in September, after which it slowly started to recede (Janssen 1987). The inundation washed the land of salts, soaked the fields, and left behind a layer of fertile silt – an optimal preparation for a successful agricultural exploitation of the land. Until 1970, when the Aswan Dam put an end to this natural phenomenon along the northernmost section of river, life along the Nile proceeded for millennia following this annual cycle; the ancient Egyptian year was in fact divided into three seasons – *akhet* ('inundation'), *peret* ('growth'), and *shemu* ('harvest').

It is worth remembering that Herodotos wrote that 'geometry' (the measurement of the land) had been invented in Egypt out of the annual necessity of re-measuring all the fields that had been covered by the inundation, and had later moved to Greece (Hdt. 2.108–109). The inundation represented the most important event of every year, a crucial period during which the near future of the population and the stability of the state were potentially challenged (Butzer 1976: 27–33; Hassan 1997): a low inundation would not reach the farthest fields, whereas an extremely high one would sweep away goods and food supplies. If this happened once or twice, it would have resulted in local problems; if, however, this happened for several years consecutively, the impact would have been potentially catastrophic, leading to famine and political unrest.

For this reason, the level of the waters was closely monitored and recorded since the earliest times. The Palermo Stone and relating fragment record the most important events that took place during the reigns of the Egyptian kings from just before the First to the Fifth Dynasty (Wilkinson 1999: 64–5). Each row refers to a different king; hieroglyphic signs for 'regnal year' divide the horizontal band into vertical spaces, each in turn divided in two: the upper part contains the most important event that took place that year, whilst the lower part records the height of the Nile (Kemp 2018: 62), clearly a matter of fundamental importance for the royal power. Altogether, the entries on the Palermo Stone provide information on the inundation levels for a period of about five hundred years (Bell 1970).

Throughout all of ancient Egyptian history, the level of the Nile was monitored with the aid of specific constructions called Nilometres. They generally consist of flights of steps that descend in the vicinity of the river, under the water's edge (Wilkinson 2000: 73); the most famous examples are the ones located on the island of Elephantine and the spectacular medieval building located on the Island of Roda in Cairo (Ghaleb 1951). In this building the inscriptions on the central pillar clearly reflect the correspondence between the inundation level and the welfare of the country. The ideal flood averaged 16–17 cubits; at 18 cubits agricultural production would have been sufficient for two years, whereas at 19–20 it cubits would have been disastrous. Seemingly, floods below 15 cubits would have seriously affected the irrigation process. According to various medieval sources, 16 cubits represented the minimum threshold for the Sultan to raise taxes on agricultural production; one author describes the taxation at 16 cubits as 'complete' and that at 17 as 'perfect' (Sandri 2017; Popper 1951: 78–82).

Until the construction of the Aswan Dam, the strict interdependency between power and floods meant that success depended on a favourable combination between the natural fluctuations of the intensity of the event and the ability of the ruler to handle the situation. In the Pharaonic period, if one of the two factors failed, *ma'at* would be disrupted and disaster would eventually strike the country.

Both the Old and the Middle Kingdom, periods of strong, centralised power, were followed by troubled Intermediate periods; in both cases, climatic and environmental anomalies have been cited as triggering or contributing factors, respectively a drought (with ensuing famine) and a series of anomalous floods. In her study on the climatic factors that appear to have negatively affected the last period of the Middle Kingdom, Barbara Bell observed that the portraits of the kings who ruled during the troubled Thirteenth Dynasty appear to 'express a melancholy resignation that is entirely compatible with the hypothesis that his reign and life would be terminated if the floods proved too meagre' (Bell 1975: 266). Even if the available evidence for the occurrence of substantial climate changes is not conclusive (Moeller 2005), it is clear that the pharaohs were aware of the dangers, regardless of the nature of the trigger, of spiralling downwards in the case of disruption of the overall balance.

Death and rebirth

Dealing with the natural cycle of life and death occupies most of human existence, in a more or less direct way. Different cultures construct different symbolic structures to deal with it, inspired by nature to various degrees. The case of ancient Egypt is peculiar, as there, environment, territory, and landscape overlapped to the point of being basically inseparable. The usual daily cycle of the sun and the annual rhythm of the seasons were interwoven with the annual cycle of the inundations and dominated by the prepossessing presence of the river. The overarching cosmological order contained an inextricable combination of geo-graphical elements, in their literal sense of being descriptions of the surroundings.

The main elements regulating the world were the water and the sun, their coordinated movements and their interactions.

Every year, the water submerged most of the country, obliterating vast areas around the settlements. When it started to recede, the land started to reappear as mounds, which became progressively larger and taller, and eventually re-emerged completely, ready to flourish again. This situation is perfectly simplified and represented by the ancient Egyptian creation myth, that saw a primeval hill rising from a dark watery substance, and then the sun rising either directly from it or from a lotus flower (Salah 1969). After the world took shape, the primeval water continued to exist around its edges, and kept feeding the Nile river (Pinch 2002: 58).

The annual cycle of the inundation and the natural cycle of life and death overlapped to the point of being coincident; this relationship was embodied in the long-lasting myth of Osiris. The eldest son of the earth god Geb and the sky goddess Nut, Osiris was murdered by his brother Seth, then cut into pieces that were scattered throughout Egypt. Osiris' wife Isis patiently retrieved all the pieces, restored the completeness of her husband's body, and conceived their son Horus, who would later avenge his dead father. Osiris was generally represented as wrapped in a white garment, his feet united, the mirror image of a mummy; his skin was usually green, hinting at the putrefaction of the flesh, as well as at the rebirth of the vegetation. The strict link between death and rebirth is also indicated by the symbolic association of all liquids issued by his body, including those relating to putrefaction, with the waters of the inundation, loaded with rotting organic material dragged along by the swollen river (Pinch 2002: 178–80).

The entire myth is imbued with references to one of the major fears of the ancient Egyptians, that is, the dismembering and decomposition of the unity of the body. This process could be avoided thanks to the mummification process, which in itself involved the partial mutilation and subsequent reconstruction of various body parts – a process of dismembering and recomposition similar to the one endured by Osiris. Every person who died, in a way, met Osiris' fate, and joined him in the Underworld (Hare 1999: 22–7).

The sun, with its powerful and pervasive presence, played a central role in the ancient Egyptian perception and description of the surrounding world. The sunset represented a dramatic transition from clear daylight to scary darkness: people would fall into a sleep similar to death, and the sun would embark on a perilous journey across the twelve hours of the night, during which it had to fight and repel ill-intentioned monsters (Wilkinson 2000: 206–7). In the New Kingdom version of the cosmographic texts, the unification of the sun with the figure of Osiris became more explicit, thus fusing life and death and closing the circle that linked them (Darnell 2004). Every night the sun would overcome all the dangers, and rise again at dawn, thus representing rebirth after death.

The hieroglyph for the word 'horizon', *akhet*, represented the sun rising between two rounded peaks, that is, what the ancient Egyptians saw every morning, when the sun rose behind the hills of the Eastern Desert. The rising sun was thus the symbol of the rebirth that took place after the dark hours of the night, into which the sun had plunged at sunset. Sunset and sunrise therefore corresponded to two opposite points of the same circle, and one recalled the other. This is probably the reason why Khufu called his pyramid, located on the western shore of the Nile and meant to lead and preserve him into the afterlife, 'the Horizon of Khufu'.

And it might also be one of the reasons why Akhenaten chose to be buried in the deep *wadi* that interrupts the escarpment that surrounded to the east the plain where his new capital had been built. The city bore the name of *akhetaten*, literally 'the horizon of Aten', the Aten being the disk of the sun. A series of so-called 'boundary stele' were carved in the rocks of the escarpment that surrounded the vast territory sacred to the Aten, including the inhabited part on the eastern shore and the hills behind it, as well as the vast cultivated area on the western shore of the Nile (Kemp 2012: 32–40). A text engraved on three of them explains that the city of Akhetaten, the 'horizon of Aten', would never be extended beyond these limits (Earlier Proclamation VII-B).

The tomb of Akhenaten himself is the only royal burial located on the eastern shore of the Nile, and its position in the eastern *wadi* might contain a meaningful message. The line of the eastern horizon runs high along the edge of the scarp but then descends to design a hollow in correspondence to the mouth of the *wadi*. Seen from the city, twice a year (in October and February) for a few days in a row the sun would be seen rising from this hollow, thus designing a gigantic *akhet* sign in the landscape (Kemp 2012: 94 and figure VI; Magli 2013: 208–14). The king, thus, planned to be buried under – actually *into* – this huge materialisation of the horizon, in which the landscape became a symbol of rebirth.

The alignment to the sun at dawn appears to have been a characteristic shared by a number of temples. The most famous cases are the temple of Abu Simbel (facing east), where the sun penetrates into the deepest sanctuary twice a year, in October and February, and the Temple of Karnak (facing west), where the sun rises along the axis marked by the sequence of pylons at the Winter Solstice (Magli 2013: 164–5). A significant number of temples were oriented eastwards within the range of movement of the sun along the horizon during the year, and therefore the phenomenon seen at Abu Simbel is likely to have taken place in several other temples as well (Shaltout and Belmonte 2005; Belmonte and Shaltout 2006; Shaltout, Belmonte, and Fekhri 2007a, 2007b).

We do not know whether the dates in which this event took place always had a meaning, as the astronomical alignment is not the only factor that influenced the direction of the temple axes, that might depend also on other factors, such as the topography or their proximity to the river. At any rate, it is a fact that twice a year the sun would align with the axis of a large number of Egyptian temples. In all the cases in which the temples included a pylon or a sequence of pylons, in those crucial days the sun would emerge from the hollow between them and recall the image of the *akhet* (see in particular Kemp and Docherty 2019 on the specific case of the Great Aten Temple).

Since the earliest period, the kings were identified with the sun-god Ra. The Pyramid Texts engraved on the walls of the Fifth Dynasty pyramid of

Unas introduce the deceased king to the god: 'Ra-Atum, this Unas comes to you, a spirit indestructible, (...) may you cross the sky united in the dark, may you rise in lightland, the place in which you shine' (Utterance 217). Thus, the west (called *imentt*), where the sun sets, became associated with death: all royal burials, pyramids and tombs (apart from Akhenaten) were in fact built on the western shore of the Nile (Ikram 2003: 41–2).

The god Khenti-amentiu, the 'Foremost of the Westerners', was an old funerary deity venerated at the ancient town of Abydos. At some point, he became associated with Osiris, whose head was said to have been stranded there (Ikram 2003: 34–5). For this reason, many early kings were buried there (Arnold 1977: 32–40), and several later kings built temples there to celebrate their funerary cults (Wilkinson 2000: 143–8). Among them, stand the impressive remains of the complex built by the Nineteenth Dynasty pharaoh Seti I, which also included a cenotaph. The latter, a stone structure sunken below ground level, consisted of a pillared hall containing a pseudo-sarcophagus on a raised platform surrounded by a trench that could be filled by water, and thus resemble the primeval mound and its powerful message of resurrection (Frankfort, De Buck, and Gunn 1933; Brand 2000: 174–8). It is even possible that the building was surmounted by an artificial hill, rising from the surrounding ground level, thus underlying its identification with the primeval mound (Wilkinson 2000: 36).

The same principle might have guided the construction of the once great mortuary temple of Amenhotep III, located on Luxor's West Bank. Differently from all the other mortuary temples, built on a higher level at a certain distance from the river, this large complex was probably meant to be invaded by the inundation, which would leave only the sanctuary standing as an island (Wilkinson 2000: 188–9). Unfortunately, this fascinating condition is likely to have quickly resulted in damage to the temple's structure, which was abandoned and largely dismantled in ancient times. In its heyday, the temple of Amenhotep III probably materialised what most temples only hinted at: the plant-shaped columns of the hypostyle halls represented the marshes where the gods were (re)born, and the innermost sanctuary contained the statue of the god on a pedestal representing the primeval mound (Pinch 2002: 21–2).

Indirect references to the presence of water can be found also in the architecture of the royal tombs of the Valley of the Kings. The deep shaft that interrupted the sequence of descending corridors in the earliest tombs has been interpreted either as a practical system to discourage thieves or to absorb flash floods, or as a symbolic representation of either the burial of Osiris or Sokar, or as the subterranean aquatic region described in the *Amduat*, the funerary text describing the nocturnal journey of the sun (Weeks 2016: 106–7). As it is often the case with ancient Egyptian art and architecture, tracing a neat line dividing practical from symbolic reasons is difficult; however, the fact that shafts stopped being quarried when the slope of the tombs was greatly reduced, suggests that they might have indeed played a role in relation to flash floods, which were less likely to be disruptive if the tomb developed horizontally (Rossi 2004: 140–1).

With or without the involvement of water, 'primeval mounds' of sand might have been built as a basement for the predynastic temples at Hierakonpolis (Quibell and Green 1902), and as parts of the Old Kingdom temple at Medamud (Robichon and Varille 1940). Among the vast artistic production on this theme, it is worth mentioning the wooden portrait of Tutankhamun: his head comes out from a lotus flower, growing from a green mound; the whole composition clearly referred to the process of rebirth of the vegetation from the primeval mound (Reeves 1990: 66).

The ancient Egyptian language and writing system played their role in the creation of symbolic and practical interconnections. The pyramidion, that is the uppermost part of obelisks and pyramids, was called *benbenet*, a feminine form of *benben*, the name of an elongated, roughly pointed stone that represented the focus of the solar cult of Heliopolis (Kemp 2018: 142). Two explanations have been suggested for this name. One is that it derived from the verb *weben* (to shine): the pyramidia of pyramids were often decorated with solar motifs, and were the first points to be illuminated by the sun at dawn and the last to be abandoned by the setting sun in the evening (Rossi 1999, 2004: 182–4); pyramidia of obelisks were even covered by sheets of gold or electrum, that 'captured' the sun in the morning and kept it shining on top of the obelisks all day long (Habachi 1977: 47–8). The other explanation is that the word might derive from the root *ben* or *bel*, a word with a sexual meaning connected with the creation of the primeval mound, called *benenet*; whether these word-games reflect an actual common origin or whether they were generated *ex post* is difficult to tell (Baines 1970).

At any rate, we are left with a dense network of references to the life-death cycle exemplified and symbolised by the relationship between water, land, and sun, the most important physical elements that may be used to describe the ancient Egyptian environment.

Water and sand

Sailing on changing waters

In the Egyptian language, the action of sailing could be expressed by three different verbs: the generic 'to sail' (on the river and at sea), and the more specific 'to sail northwards/downstream' and 'to sail southwards/upstream'. These two actions corresponded to two completely different methods:

sailing northwards took advantage of the stream, whereas sailing southwards relied on the prevailing wind, which blows from the north. This difference is clearly visible in the ancient hieroglyphs used to describe them since the earliest times: the verb 'to travel northward' (not necessarily on water) was accompanied by the representation of a boat with its sails folded down, whilst 'to travel southwards' was followed by a boat with open sails (Shaw and Nicholson 2008: 302–3).

Until relatively recent times, sailing along the Nile was the fastest and most efficient way to travel along the Valley. When Egypt became part of the Roman Empire, the Romans extended to this country their state-run transport and communication system called *cursus publicus*, but added a special service that did not exist elsewhere called *cursus velox*, that exploited the fast track offered by the Nile river (Kolb 2001: 100).

As the first and foremost travelling method in Egypt, sailing played an important role in religious tales and ceremonies (Ward 2000): the sun-god crossed the night on a boat, sacred representations of gods were paraded on boats along the Nile (Görg 2001), and the souls of the dead reached the netherworld on boats. In the Old and Middle Kingdoms, large boats were carefully dismantled and buried in dedicated pits near some major royal pyramids (Lehner 1997: 80, 109, 118–9, 155; Arnold 2002: 106–7). The most famous is one of the two solar boats of Khufu, which was laboriously re-assembled and placed on display in a specifically designed museum near its finding spot (Lipke 1984), and that has now been moved to the Grand Egyptian Museum. These boats might have been used to transport the king's body to his final destination, to be then buried with him and used in his journey in the afterlife (Landström 1970: 90–3).

For four months a year, during the inundation, the importance and role of sailing became even more pronounced: the flood dramatically changed the appearance of the Nile Valley, which became similar to a large lake dotted by islands. Although a number of roads running on embankments probably remained above water, the bulk of transport shifted from pack animals to boats; these could move along shortcuts and more direct itineraries in comparison with most of the roads, that must avoid obstacles and irregularities of the landscape (cf. Hdt. 2.97). It was during this season that most of the stones, heavy building material, and monolithic monuments were transported by boat not only up and down the Nile, but also east and west to the farthest points reached by the inundation, in order to approach the building sites of royal monuments (Arnold 1991: 57–66). These transport barges were able to sustain significant loads: a representation on the wall of the Temple of Queen Hatshepsut at Deir al-Bahari shows two large obelisks loaded side by side on a boat (cf. Clarke and Engelbach 1930: chapter IV).

The construction of stone temples and funerary complexes must have implied the transport and arrival to the building site of large amounts of material, actions that had to be timed by combining the necessities of the builders with the inundation period (cf. Tallet 2017). The desert edge from Giza to Saqqara is punctuated by evidence pointing to the existence of basins and piers, where probably the large barges discharged their loads destined to the pyramid complexes that were being built on top of the plateau (e.g. Lehner 1997: 82–3); the blocks were then dragged on the desert surface along ramps sometimes reinforced with timber (Arnold 1991: 79–98).

The Giza plateau was also reached by the inundation: some early XX century pictures, taken before the construction of the Aswan Dam, show the Giza pyramids reflected upside down in the flooded land. In this case, however, the floodwater might have been too shallow to be navigated by heavy-loaded barges, and the transport of building material is likely to have relied on a number of canals, probably also used to irrigate the area (Butzer 1976: 45–6).

The funerary complexes of Old and Middle Kingdom consisted of a pyramid (accompanied by a tiny satellite pyramid and a varying number of small pyramids for the queens), a mortuary temple located next to the pyramid on high ground and a Valley temple located down at the edges of the cultivation, connected to the mortuary temple by a ceremonial ramp (Lehner 1997: 18–9). From pictorial and textual evidence, we know that the body of the dead king was transported by boat to the docking area, where he underwent the mummification process before being transported up to the pyramid (Lehner 1997: 25–7). Thus, both the construction works and the elaborate burial ceremony followed the same sequence: the arrival by boat to the docking area, the preparation, and the transport up onto the plateau to the final destination.

Most of the travelling that took place along or across the river had a symbolic counterpart in the religious and funerary realms. Different was the case of long-distance travels carried out for military or commercial reasons, that implied facing the different and specific dangers of sailing at sea. Since the Fifth Dynasty, the Egyptians organised expeditions to the land of Punt, probably located in the area of the Horn of Africa and modern Yemen, which could be reached after a relatively safe coastal journey, departing from the harbours located along the Red Sea coast (Creasman and Doyle 2017; Hense and Sidebotham 2017; Hense, Kaper, and Geest 2016; Sidebotham, Hense, and Nouwens 2008: 151–6; Trigger et al. 1983: 136–7, 270–1). This type of journey, long and complex, was clearly not commonplace and represented a significant achievement for both the kings who had the power to order them and the officers in charge of completing them successfully, who proudly recorded them on the walls of their tombs.

Marching across the deserts

If travelling on water represented a significant portion of the ancient Egyptian short- and long-range movements, travelling on sand played its own important role (Mumford 2017): marching from water source to water source in the deserts was the only way to keep under control the vast areas that bordered the Valley on either side, and required a completely different organisation in comparison with sailing.

In a scale of possible dangers, sailing along the Nile was certainly safer than sailing at sea, where the dangers of getting lost, and of incurring inclement weather and lack of drinking water had to be taken into account. Travelling in the deserts posed similar problems, but in completely different environmental conditions: venturing towards distant destinations meant bringing along all the necessary water and food, which had to be transported by men and pack animals. Donkeys represented the main transport means until the introduction of camels, that became widespread in the Graeco-Roman period (Kuhrt 1999; Boessneck 1988).

Two interesting sources offer important information on desert travels in ancient Egypt: the account of the travels of Harkhuf, and the only extant ancient Egyptian topographic map.

Harkhuf was an Upper Egyptian governor who served under the pharaohs Merenra and Pepi II, rulers of the Old Kingdom Sixth Dynasty. Around 2280 BCE he travelled to the land of Yam, located somewhere to the south of Egypt, and left a detailed account of his expeditions on the walls of his tomb in Aswan (Lichtheim 1973: 23–7). Harkhuf was sent to open a commercial route, and also to explore the territory and the possible travel itineraries. It is worth reading his own account of these travels, which offers a vivid description of the length and complexity of such an enterprise:

> The Majesty of Merenra, my lord, sent me together with my father, the Sole Companion and Lector-Priest Iri, to Yam to open the way to the country. I did it in seven months; I brought from it all kinds of beautiful and rare gifts, and was praised for it very greatly. His majesty sent me a second time alone. I went up on the Yebu road and came down via Mekher, Terers and Irtjetj (…) in the space of eight months. I came down bringing gifts from that country in great quantity, the likes of which had never before been brought back to this land. I came down through the region of the house of the chief of Setju and Irtjet, I explored those foreign lands. (…) Then his majesty sent me a third time to Yam. I went up from the *nome* of This upon the Oasis road. (…) I came down with three hundred donkeys laden with incense, ebony,

hekenw-oil, sat, panther skins, elephant's tusks, throw sticks, and all sorts of good products.

(Autobiography of Harkhuf, right side of entrance 4–14, left side of entrance 1–4)

The precise position of the land of Yam is unclear and has been the subject of a long debate (for a summary, see Cooper 2012). At any rate, it appears that in the Old Kingdom the ancient Egyptians travelled extensively across the desert and entertained significant commercial relationships with central Africa. Nothing is known of how Harkhuf and other ancient Egyptian travellers of that period recorded their itineraries. Clearly, official journeys organised in the name of the king and that also involved the transport of precious gifts were carefully organised in advance: the number of people and donkeys, their load, the number of marching days, everything must have been planned in advance on the basis of previous knowledge of the routes, which must have been somehow recorded and transmitted.

The second source is the only extant ancient Egyptian topographical map (Museo Egizio, Torino cat. 1879 and relating fragments), which dates to about 1,100 years later: drawn on a sheet of papyrus, it represents the itinerary to reach the mining settlement of Umm al-Fawakhir in the Eastern Desert (Baud 1990). The map shows a track running along a sequence of desert *wadis* bordered by high peaks, drawn flat on either side of the valleys; annotations in hieratic offer further information on locations and directions (Gardiner 1914; Shore 1987: 121–4), and the various stones of which the mountains are made are clearly indicated by different patterns (Harrell and Brown 1992).

The combination of drawing and written indications, which can also be found in ancient Egyptian architectural drawings (Rossi 2004: 96–113), represents an efficient way to convey all the information that travellers need: in this respect, the Eastern Desert map is a precursor of the later Roman *itineraria non tantum adnotata sed etiam picta* ('itineraries not only annotated but also illustrated') that were used over 1,100 years later (thus c. 2,200 years after Harkhuf, Rossi 2012). It would not be surprising to find out that travels on land relied for millennia on the same efficient combination of drawn and written descriptions of the earth.

Dominating the landscape

We know very little of the ancient Egyptian ability to survey large territories, apart from the fact that they did it. Perhaps the use of the term 'survey' should be avoided, as we immediately think of measuring the land and representing it on a map; we could speak instead of a process of physical acquaintance with the terrain, and of the ensuing possibility to exploit and dominate it, with or without involving measurements and map-making.

The ancient Egyptians clearly had a penchant for large-scale architectural projects, as attested since the earliest times by their imposing funerary complexes: the action of levelling the basement of a pyramid, for instance, represented a significant task, especially when the pyramid itself was built around a rock core, as was the case of that of Khufu at Giza. The ancient builders measured the distances by means of cords, subdivided by knots or painted marks (Rossi 2004: 154); horizontal planes were established using a square level (Arnold 1991: 13), water running in trenches, or reference lines (Lehner 1997: 214–5); vertical lines were established by plumb bobs.

The same combination of simple tools was employed in land management. The scale of artificial irrigation in ancient Egypt is disputed: the existence of artificial canals is taken for granted, but their actual extent is unclear. Digging canals was probably one element of a more complex group of activities; in his pioneering work *Early Hydraulic Civilization in Egypt*, Butzer concluded that irrigation technology in the Dynastic period was:

> geared primarily towards regulation of the high-water Nile: conversion of the natural to higher and stronger artificial levees; enlarging and dredging of natural diverging overflow channels; blocking off of natural, gathering or drainage channels by earthen dams and sluice gates; subdivision of the flood basins by dams into manageable, in part special-purpose, units; and controlling water access to and retention in the basin subunits by temporary cuts in the levees or dikes or by a network of short canals and masonry gates.
>
> (Butzer 1976: 47)

His view has been substantially confirmed by recent studies (Antoine 2017; Willems et al. 2017). All these operations were probably based on how water moved on the terrain during the inundation (cf. Römer 2017). The receding tide highlighted the presence of shallow areas and slopes that channelled the waters, and probably suggested which modifications should be implemented to achieve specific results. In other words, in the areas affected by the annual inundation, the use of survey instruments might have been restricted to relatively small areas or to establishing shapes and boundaries, rather than to understanding the overall conformation of the terrain.

Measurements, in fact, can even get in the way of large-scale projects if they are wrong, as happened for the Suez Canal: the Napoleonic project of connecting the Mediterranean and the Red Sea with a channel running in a north–south direction remained at a standstill for decades because, piecing together partial surveys of the area, the engineers had concluded that there was a drop of 10 m between the two seas, to be solved with the construction of expensive locks (Wilson 1939).

The idea of establishing a navigable watercourse ending in the Red Sea was an old Egyptian idea, dating back perhaps to the Middle Kingdom, implemented in the Late Period (Redmount 1995) and later probably reprised by the Roman emperor Trajan. However, the ancient Egyptian canal had a completely different function, that of connecting *their* major thoroughfare, the Nile, with the Red Sea. This was achieved by exploiting the ancient distributary of the river that used to flow eastwards along the modern Wadi Tumilat, in the direction of the chain of lakes that once probably marked the shoreline of the Red Sea (Wilson 1939: 4). The connection with the Mediterranean was ensured by all the other navigable canals crossing the Delta. The same sequence of lakes was later exploited by the modern Suez Canal, that 'cut' across the eastern corner of the Delta in a north–south direction to create a direct connection with the Mediterranean, thus making the transition quicker and bypassing the control that Egypt could exercise on people and goods.

In ancient times Wadi Tumilat, too, was flooded by the annual inundation: therefore, the ancient works to construct a navigable canal there did not necessarily require large-scale measurements, only the observation of how the water moved along it. Once more, the actions to be performed were planned and acted as a corollary to a major natural event, which was part of a pervasive, large-scale order.

Division and unification

The two countries

According to the ancient Egyptians, their state was created by the unification of Upper Egypt (the Nile Valley) and Lower Egypt (the Delta) by the first king, traditionally called Menes. The official king lists, periodically compiled and recorded on stone or papyrus, conveyed an impression of continuity and linear order, which was highly regarded by the ancient Egyptians (Redford 1986; cf. Assmann 2011: 3). Menes appears as the first name, and is followed by a uniform, continuous sequence of other kings; rulers who did not conform to this linear narrative, including Akhenaten (who introduced a significant religious change) or Hatshepsut (a woman), were carefully excluded (Kemp 2018: 59–63).

The oldest source telling the tale of Egypt's unification is the Narmer palette, a votive object found in the temple of Hierakonpolis (Quibell 1900); its two sides show two parts of the same story, the conquest of Lower Egypt by the Upper Egyptian king called Narmer, that took place around 3000 BCE (Wilkinson 1999: 67–70). The first scene represents the king, wearing the

White Crown associated to Upper Egypt, brandishing a mace-head over a defeated man, represented with hair and beard of Libyan style. In the second scene, Narmer, wearing this time the Red Crown of Lower Egypt, marches together with a series of figures holding standards, evidently representing the winning coalition. The dramatic scene to the right does not leave any doubt as to the violence of the war: two rows of defeated enemies lie on the ground, their arms tied, and their severed heads placed between their legs. The central portion of this side is occupied by two lions, restrained by two men, their long necks intertwined in a design reminiscent of Mesopotamian artistic representations.

According to the representations on this palette, the story goes that the king of Upper Egypt conquered Lower Egypt and unified the country. This corresponds, broadly speaking, to the core of the events; however, the archaeological evidence dating to this period points to a slightly more complex scenario. It seems that a constellation of small communities scattered along the Nile converged into a single state, in the space of just 300–400 years (Wilkinson 1999: 44–52). It was probably the city of Hierakonpolis, located in Upper Egypt, that managed to overcome all the others and expand along the Nile, both to the south and to the north (Kemp 2018: 70–5).

The fact that the establishment of the unified Egyptian state brought a turbulent period to its end and established a general order left a lasting impression on the Egyptians: scenes in which chaotic masses are being contained by powerful figures continued to be represented for centuries (Kemp 2018: 89–97). In the Hypostyle Hall of the Karnak Temple, for instance, dating to nearly 1,700 years after the birth of the Egyptian state, the king Ramses II and the gods Horus and Khnum are depicted capturing wild fowls in a papyrus marsh. The disordered mass of the birds trapped in the net marks a stark contrast with the rest of the scene, in which the parallel papyrus stems provide a neat background to the symmetric trap, firmly held by the three holy figures striking a choreographic pose.

Shaped (in different ways) by the same element (water), Upper and Lower Egypt were different, and yet belonged to and in fact constituted the state in the only form that was acceptable to the ancient Egyptians: as the unity of two entities.

The two powers

The creation of the Egyptian state from the unification of two powers remained a fundamental concept throughout the entire ancient Egyptian history. Among the five traditional names of the pharaohs, the second was the *nebty*-name; *nebty* means 'two ladies' and refers to the patron goddesses of Upper and Lower Egypt. The third name, today known as the 'prenomen', could be preceded by two titles: one was *nisw-bity*, generally translated as 'King of Upper and Lower Egypt' but that should be more precisely rendered as the 'Two-Aspected King'; the other was *neb-tawy*, 'Lord of the Two Lands' (Dodson and Hilton 2004: 11).

The contraposition of two powers transpires from the earliest kings' names and titles. The two lions of the Narmer palette and Tomb 100 at Hierakonpolis generically represented two equal powers harmonically combined into one unit, whilst a more explicit representation directly referring to the Egyptian state is the pair of Horus falcons facing one another on top of the *serekh* of some predynastic rulers. The names of some Second Dynasty kings are particularly interesting: the name of the first, Hetepsekhemwy, means 'The Two Powers Are in Peace'; very little is known about this ruler and the two powers to which he refers in his name are not known. One of the following kings, Peribsen, chose to write his name in a *serekh* surmounted by the dog-like Seth animal; no other king ever did the same. Perhaps this king only reigned over part of the country associated with this god, but the scarcity of historical sources prevents us from drawing final conclusions (Wilkinson 1999: 89–90).

The dynasty closed with Khasekhem, whose name meant 'The-Power-Appears'. This king later changed his name into the dual form Khasekhemwy, 'The-Two-Powers-Appear', and added the epithet 'The-Two-Lords-Are-at-Peace-with-Him'. This change of name might represent a ritual reference to the birth of the Egyptian state, or it might refer to actual contrasts between opposed powers (Wilkinson 1999: 89–94). To Khasekhemwy belongs a *serekh* in which the king's name is surmounted by two figures, the falcon Horus and the dog-like Seth (Kemp 2018: 96).

In Egyptian mythology Horus and Seth had a complex, conflictual, and ambiguous relationship. They are either described as brothers or as nephew and uncle, so they are somehow bound by family ties. Since his birth, Seth disrupted the order and clashed repeatedly with Horus. The god Thoth separated them and what they represented: order from disorder, 'heaven and earth, earth and underworld, right and left, black and red, to be born and to be conceived, rulership and strength, life and dominion' (Te Velde 1967: 60).

Whether or not the contrast between Horus and Seth directly reflected the contest between two groups of inhabitants of the region for the rule over the entire Valley is difficult to establish (Te Velde 1967: 74–80). Horus is often associated with Lower Egypt and Seth with Upper Egypt, but according to the Narmer palette it was Upper Egypt that conquered Lower Egypt. It has been suggested that this duality reflects an even earlier contrast that might have taken place in Upper Egypt before the conquest of Lower Egypt, between the two cities of Hierakonpolis, where Horus was worshipped, and Naqada, associated instead with Seth (Melzer 2002).

A hint that a strict association with a north–south division of the Valley is not an exhaustive explanation is offered by the fact that Seth was also associated with the desert, where he was banned – or at least this is what the Valley-centric tales say. The population of the oases, on their side, worshipped him for centuries, as a powerful god able to bring fertility to the local land (Bagnall and Tallet 2019: 11).

The overall impression is that Horus and Seth represented two sides of the same coin, that is, the two halves of a unit that, in order to exist, needed the comparative contrast with one another. Upper and Lower Egypt existed in relation to one another, the Valley was defined by the presence of the deserts, order distinguished itself from disorder. Egypt, as a whole, was defined by pairs of elements which did not fuse together, but equally collaborated and contributed to its definition in a balanced way.

It all comes together

In ancient Egypt, the presence of pairs was a founding and persistent concept: the number one corresponded to the initial lack of differentiation of the primeval water, before 'two things existed' (Dunand and Zivie-Coche 2004: 32–3). Therefore, it took two to make an identifiable unit (cf. Assmann 2011: 147–9). The crown worn by all Egyptian kings from the early dynastic to the latest period reflects this process: the so-called Double Crown, consisting of a combination of the White Crown of Upper Egypt with the Red Crown of Lower Egypt, was called *sekhem-ty*, 'the two powerful ones', and was decorated by a cobra (known as *uraeus*) and a vulture, symbols of the goddesses of Lower and Upper Egypt, the 'two ladies' of the king's title.

The king, with his crowns, names, and titles, kept the country united; the death of a king represented a dangerous moment in which the original divisions could resurface and threaten the stability of the state. Normally, this crisis was just theoretical and would be soon dispelled by the crowning of a new king. Sometimes, however, these transitions did not proceed smoothly, and the much-dreaded fragmentation of the country did take place, not necessarily between Upper and Lower Egypt, but among a scatter of local powers (as happened in the First Intermediate Period) or at the hands of foreign invaders (as happened in the Second Intermediate Period, cf. Kemp 2018: 64–6). Once the central power was restored, by kings who gained everlasting fame and respect for their achievement, spurious kings belonging to minor dynasties were carefully expunged from the official chronicles and king lists to be engraved on the temple walls.

The unification of the Egyptian state was recalled and celebrated by elaborated representations showing Horus and Seth tying together a lotus and a papyrus, the heraldic plants of Upper and Lower Egypt, around the hieroglyphic sign for 'unification'. The name of the king, standing on top of the latter, represented the final seal to this operation (Kemp 2018: 66–70). If we also consider the association of Seth with the deserts, then the traditional Egyptian representation of the country's unification is really complete: north, south, east, west, valley, and desert all tied together symmetrically by the reassuring power of the pharaoh.

Unity was the key to success, and symbols reflect reality: in ancient times, for an estimated population fluctuating between one and three million (cf. Butzer 1976: chapter 7), keeping under control an elongated country subject to a major natural event every year was a complex task to be faced collectively, by joining all available forces. One of the few surviving representations of the early king 'Scorpion' depicts him brandishing a plough, in the act of working at the junction between two canals (Wilkinson 1999: 56–7); this is the earliest representation of artificial irrigation in ancient Egypt (Butzer 1976: 20–1). The successful management of water and land represented the most important task for all the Egyptians, symbolically starting from the king himself, who represented the core of the Egyptian state and the key to its stability.

The automatic association between large-scale maintenance of hydraulic systems and authoritarian systems posed by some authors has been challenged by the evidence that piecemeal management of water resources could be achieved locally, without massive, centralised, state intervention (Horden and Purcell 2000: 249–51). Eyre (1994), for instance, noted that in ancient Egypt private landowners who could afford it invested in improving the productivity of their land even more than the central state, and Butzer (1976: 51) observed that 'dynastic irrigation was naturally compartmentalised, so that a centralized administration was neither practicable nor purposeful'.

At any rate, both the central state and the private owners worked towards the same goal: exploiting the potentially risky interaction between the flood and the cultivable land in the best possible way. Governing the effects of a massive flood required large-scale cooperation and the collaboration of all the actors involved, who thus worked separately but to the same shared purpose. The unification of Egypt was embodied by its defining element: the river, along which everything moved and rotated. And the river, in turn, was linked to the rest of the world by precise spatial and rhythmic connections, respectively, the cardinal points and the daily and annual cycles.

All this took place within the horizon of the visible world, as seen from the Valley. So, regardless of the passing of centuries and the shifting religious connotations, the reassuring symmetry and interdependence between sunset and sunrise, and therefore death and rebirth, continued to inspire and shape the minds of the ancient Egyptians. All lines were closed in circles, all events belonged to cycles. The description of the earth contained all the necessary clues to inhabit the land, exploit its resources, and keep the power.

The position, orientation, design, and organisation of funerary and religious buildings represent a tangible trace of how mindset and landscape interact with each other. Temples would come to life every morning when the sunrays penetrated along their axis or rose behind their pylons; the peaks of obelisks and pyramids would make the most of the daylight; and colourful representations of the life of people, flora, and fauna along the busy shores of the Nile accompanied the dead in the darkness of their tombs. Ancient Egyptian culture, as expressed through texts, art, and architecture, may be defined as deeply geo-graphical, as it constantly referred to the surrounding territory, landscape, and environment. The most meaningful and powerful image able to summarise this deep connection is that of the personified sun sailing on a boat at night: a human version of a celestial body travelling on terrestrial waters in an invisible, mirror world.

In conclusion, the ancient Egyptian civilisation was born, evolved, and rhythmically functioned in synchrony with the seasonal cycles, in a continuum that included and merged practical and symbolic aspects. This environmentally self-contained and geographically self-referential nucleus was provided by strong tentacles that stretched far from the core to reach specific destinations and bring back home wealth and glory. Major maritime and land expeditions were just the peak of regular trading activities that occurred since the earliest period. The intention here is not to support the view of an 'isolated' Egypt that had little contact with the outer world, but rather to highlight how all these movements were strongly centripetal: they did not imply an appropriation of land and were meant to increase the power and wealth of the core of the system. In this respect, Greek civilisation experienced, occupied, and exploited the space in a completely different way, as we shall see in the next chapter.

Bibliographical references

Primary sources

Autobiography of Harkhuf. English translation from Lichtheim M. 1973. *Ancient Egyptian Literature. Vol. I: The Old and Middle Kingdoms*. Berkley/Los Angeles/London, University of California Press: 25–6.

Earlier Proclamation from the boundary stele of Akhenaten. English translation in Murnane J. W and Van Siclen C. C. 2011. *The Boundary Stele of Akhenaten*. London, Routledge: chapter 2.

First hymn to the sun-god from the stele of Suti and Hor. English translation from Lichtheim M. 1976. *Ancient Egyptian Literature. Vol. II: The New Kingdom*. Berkley/Los Angeles/London, University of California Press: 86–9.

Hdt.: Herodotus, *Historiae*. English translation from the Perseus Digital Library (perseus.tufts.edu).
Pyramid Texts. English translation from Lichtheim M. 1973. *Ancient Egyptian Literature. Vol. I: The Old and Middle Kingdoms*. Berkley/Los Angeles/London, University of California Press: 29–50.

Secondary sources

Antoine J.-Ch. 2017. 'Modelling the Nile Agricultural Floodplain in Eleventh and Tenth Century B.C. Middle Egypt: A Study of the P. Wilbour and Other Land Registers', in H. Willems and J.-M. Dahms (eds.), *The Nile: Natural and Cultural Landscape in Egypt: Proceedings of the International Symposium held at the Johannes Gutenberg-Universität Mainz, 22 & 23 February 2013*, Bielefeld, transcript Verlag 36: 15–52.
Arnold D. 1977. 'Royal Cult Complexes of the Old and Middle Kingdoms', in B. E. Shafer (ed.), *Temples of Ancient Egypt*. London/New York, Taurus: 31–85.
Arnold D. 1991. *Building in Egypt: Pharaonic Stone Masonry*. New York/Oxford, Oxford University Press.
Arnold D. 2002. *The Pyramid Complex of Senwosret III at Dahshur: Architectural Studies*. New York, Metropolitan Museum of Art Egyptian Expedition.
Assmann J. 1990. *Ma'at: Gerechtigkeit und Unsterblichkeit im alten Ägypten*. Münich, C. H. Beck.
Assmann J. 2011. *Cultural Memory and Early Civilization: Writing, Remembrance, and Political Imagination*. Cambridge, Cambridge University Press.
Aston B., Harrell J. and Shaw I. 2000. 'Stone', in P. T. Nicholson and I. Shaw (eds.), *Ancient Egyptian Materials and Technology*. Cambridge, Cambridge University Press: 5–77.
Bagnall R. S. and Tallet G. 2019. 'Introduction', in R. S. Bagnall and G. Tallet (eds.), *The Great Oasis of Egypt: The Kharga and Dakhla Oases in Antiquity*. Cambridge, Cambridge University Press: 1–14.
Baines J. 1970. 'Benben: Mythological and Linguistic Notes', *Orientalia* 39(3): 389–404.
Baud M. 1990, 'La représentation de l'espace en Égypte ancienne: cartographie d'un itinéraire d'expédition', *Bulletin de l'Institut Français d'Archéologie Orientale* 90: 51–63.
Bell B. 1970. 'The Oldest Records of the Nile Floods', *Geographical Journal* 136.4: 569–73.
Bell B. 1975. 'Climate and the History of Egypt: The Middle Kingdom', *American Journal of Archaeology* 79.3: 223–69.
Belmonte J. and Shaltout M. 2006. 'On the Orientation of Ancient Egyptian Temples: (2) New Experiments at the Oases of the Western Desert', *Journal for the History of Astronomy* 37.2: 173–92.
Boessneck J. 1988. *Die Tierwelt des Alten Ägypten*. München, Beck.
Brand P. J. 2000. *The Monuments of Seti I: Epigraphic, Historical, and Art Historical Analysis*. Leiden, Brill.

Butzer K. W. 1976. *Early Hydraulic Civilization in Egypt: A Study in Cultural Ecology*. Chicago/London, University of Chicago Press.
Clarke S. and Engelbach R. 1930. *Ancient Egyptian Masonry: The Building Craft*. London, Milford and Oxford University Press.
Cooper J. 2012. 'Reconsidering the Location of Yam', *Journal of the American Research Center in Egypt* 48: 1–21.
Creasman P. P. and Doyle N. 2017. 'Paths in the Deep: Maritime Connections', in P. P. Creasman and R. H. Wilkinson (eds.), *Pharaoh's Land and Beyond*. Oxford, Oxford University Press: 19–34.
Darnell J. C. 2004. *The Enigmatic Netherworld Books of the Solar Osirian Unity: Cryptographic Compositions in the Tombs of Tutankhamun, Ramesses VI, and Ramesses IX*. Orbis Biblicus et Orientalis 198. Göttingen, Vandenhoeck & Ruprecht.
Dodson A. and Hilton D. 2004. *The Complete Royal Families of Ancient Egypt*. London, Thames and Hudson.
Dunand F. and Zivie-Coche C. 2004. *Gods and Men in Egypt, 3000 BCE to 395 CE*. Ithaca/London, Cornell University Press.
Eyre C. J. 1994. 'The Water Regime for Orchards and Plantations in Pharaonic Egypt', *Journal of Egyptian Archaeology* 80: 57–80.
Frankfort H., De Buck A. and Gunn B. 1933. *The Cenotaph of Seti I at Abydos, Memoir of the Egypt Exploration Society*. London, Egypt Exploration Society.
Gardiner A. H. 1914. 'The Map of the Gold Mines in a Ramesside Papyrus at Turin', *Cairo Scientific Journal* 8: 41–6.
Ghaleb K. O. 1951. *Le Mikyâs ou Nilomètre de l'Île de Rodah*. Mémoires de l'Institut d'Ègypte 54. Cairo, Institut François d'Archéologie Orientale.
Görg M. 2001. *Die Barke der Sonne: Religion im alten Ägypten*. Freiburg, Herder.
Habachi L. 1977. *The Obelisks of Egypt*. London, Scribner's Son.
Hare T. 1999. *ReMembering Osiris: Number, Gender, and the World in Ancient Egyptian Representational Systems*. Stanford, Stanford University Press.
Harrell J. A. and Brown V. M. 1992. 'The Oldest Surviving Topographical Map from Ancient Egypt (Turin Papyri 1879, 1899 and 1969)', *Journal of the American Research Center in Egypt* 29: 81–105.
Hassan F. 1997. 'The Dynamics of a Riverine Civilization: A Geoarchaeological Perspective on the Nile Valley, Egypt', *World Archaeology* 29.1: 51–74.
Hense M., Kaper O. and Geest R. 2016. 'A Stela of Amenemhet IV from the Main Temple at Berenike', *Bibliotheca Orientalis* LXXII.5/6: 585–601.
Hense M. and Sidebotham S. 2017. 'A Middle Kingdom Stela from a Graeco-Roman Red Sea Port', *Egyptian Archaeology* 51: 41–3.
Horden P. and Purcell N. 2000. *The Corrupting Sea: A Study of the Mediterranean History*. Malden/Oxford/Carlton, Blackwell Publishing.
Ikram S. 2003. *Death and Burial in Ancient Egypt*. London, Pearson.
Janssen Jac J. 1987. 'The Day the Inundation Began', *Journal of Near Eastern Studies* 46.2: 129–36.
Kemp B. J. 2012. *The City of Akhenaten and Nefertiti: Amarna and its People*. London, Thames and Hudson.
Kemp B. J. 2018. *Ancient Egypt: Anatomy of a Civilisation* (3rd revised edition). London/New York, Routledge.

Kemp B. J. and Docherty P. 2019. 'The Solar Observation and Offering Platform at the Front of the Great Aten Temple', Online Resource (www.amarnaproject.com/documents/pdf/Solar-Observation-and-Offering-Platform.pdf, 10 December 2021).
Kolb A. 2001. 'Transport and Communication in the Roman State: The cursus publicus', in C. Adams and R. Laurence (eds.), Travel and Geography in the Roman Empire. London/New York, Routledge: 95–105.
Krzyszkowska O. and Morkot R. 2000. 'Ivory and Related Materials', in P. T. Nicholson and I. Shaw (eds.), Ancient Egyptian Materials and Technology. Cambridge, Cambridge University Press: 320–31.
Kuhrt A. 1999. 'The Exploitation of the Camel in the Neo-Assyrian Empire', in A. Leahy and J. Tait (eds.), Studies on Ancient Egypt in Honour of H.S. Smith. London, Egypt Exploration Society: 179–84.
Kuper R. 2002. 'Routes and Roots in Egypt's Western Desert: The Early Holocene Resettlement of the Eastern Sahara', in R. Friedman (ed.), Egypt and Nubia: Gifts of the Desert. London, British Museum Press: 1–12.
Landström B. 1970. Ships of the Pharaohs: 4000 Years of Egyptian Shipbuilding. New York, Doubleday.
Lehner M. 1997. The Complete Pyramids. London, Thames and Hudson.
Lichtheim M. 1973. Ancient Egyptian Literature. Vol. I: The Old and Middle Kingdoms. Berkley/Los Angeles/London, University of California Press.
Lichtheim M. 1976. Ancient Egyptian Literature. Vol. I: The New Kingdom. Berkley/Los Angeles/London, University of California Press.
Lipke P. 1984. The Royal Ship of Cheops: A Retrospective Account of the Discovery, Restoration and Reconstruction. Oxford, B.A.R.
Magli G. 2013. Architecture, Astronomy and Sacred Landscape in Ancient Egypt. Cambridge, Cambridge Universtiy Press.
Meltzer E. S. 2002. 'Horus', in D. B. Redford (ed.), The Ancient Gods Speak: A Guide to Egyptian Religion. New York, Oxford University Press: 164–9.
Moeller N. 2005. 'The First Intermediate Period: A Time of Famine and Climate Change?', Ägypten und Levante 15: 153–67.
Mumford G. 2017. 'Pathways to Distant Kingdoms: Land Connections', in P. P. Creasman and R. H. Wilkinson (eds.), Pharaoh's Land and Beyond. Oxford, Oxford University Press: 35–57.
Murnane J. W and Van Siclen C. C. 2011. The Boundary Stele of Akhenaten. London, Routledge.
O'Connor D. 1993. Ancient Nubia: Egypt's Rival in Africa. Philadelphia, University of Pennsylvania Press.
Ogden J. 2000. 'Metals', in P. T. Nicholson and I. Shaw (eds.), Ancient Egyptian Materials and Technology. Cambridge, Cambridge University Press: 148–76.
Pinch G. 2002. Egyptian Mythology: A Guide to the Gods, Goddesses, and Traditions of Ancient Egypt. Oxford, Oxford University Press.
Popper W. 1951. The Cairo Nilometer: Studies in Ibn Taghrī Birdī's Chronicles of Egypt: I, University of California Publications in Semitic Philology XII. Berkeley/Los Angeles, University of California Press.
Quibell J. E. 1900. Hierakonpolis I. London, Quaritch.
Quibell J. E. and Green F. W. 1902. Hierakonpolis II. London, Quaritch.

Redford D. B. 1986. *Pharaonic King-Lists, Annals and Day-Books: A Contribution to the Study of the Egyptian Sense of History*. Mississauga, Benben Publications.
Redmount C. A. 1995. 'The Wadi Tumilat and the "Canal of the Pharaohs"', *Journal of Near Eastern Studies* 54.2: 127–35.
Reeves N. 1990. *The Complete Tutankhamun*. London, Thames and Hudson.
Robichon C. and Varille A. 1940. *Description sommaire du temple primitif de Médamoud*. Cairo, Institut Français d'Archéologie Orientale.
Römer C. 2017. 'The Nile in the Fayum: Strategies of Dominating and Using the Water Resources of the River in the Oasis in the Middle Kingdom and the Graeco-Roman Period', in H. Willems and J.-M. Dahms (eds.), *The Nile: Natural and Cultural Landscape in Egypt: Proceedings of the International Symposium held at the Johannes Gutenberg-Universität Mainz, 22 & 23 February 2013*, Bielefeld, transcript Verlag: 171–92.
Rossi C. 1999. 'Note on the Pyramidion Found at Dahshur', *Journal of Egyptian Archaeology* 85: 219–22.
Rossi C. 2004. *Architecture and Mathematics in Ancient Egypt*. Cambridge, Cambridge University Press.
Rossi C. 2012. 'Maps, Egypt', in R. S. Bagnall, K. Brodersen, C. B. Champion, A. Erskine and S. R. Huebner (eds.), *The Encyclopedia of Ancient History*. Malden, Blackwell: 4274–6.
Salah A. A. 1969. 'The So-Called "Primeval Hill" and Other Related Elevations in Ancient Egyptian Mythology', in *Mitteilungen des Deutschen Archäologischen Instituts Kairo* 25: 110–20.
Sandri S. 2017. 'Nilometers – or: Can You Measure Wealth?', in H. Willems and J.-M. Dahms (eds.), *The Nile: Natural and Cultural Landscape in Egypt: Proceedings of the International Symposium held at the Johannes Gutenberg-Universität Mainz, 22 & 23 February 2013*, Bielefeld, transcript Verlag: 193–214.
Shaltout M. and Belmonte J. 2005. 'On the Orientation of Ancient Egyptian Temples: (1) Upper Egypt and Lower Nubia', *Journal for the History of Astronomy* 36(3): 273–98.
Shaltout M., Belmonte J. and Fekhri M. 2007a. 'On the Orientation of Ancient Egyptian Temples: (3) Key Points in Lower Egypt and Siwa Oasis (Part 1)', *Journal for the History of Astronomy* 38.2: 141–60.
Shaltout M., Belmonte J. and Fekhri M. 2007b. 'On the Orientation of Ancient Egyptian Temples: (3) Key Points in Lower Egypt and Siwa Oasis (Part 2)', *Journal for the History of Astronomy* 38.4: 413–42.
Shaw I. and Nicholson P. 2008. *The Princeton Dictionary of Ancient Egypt* (revised edition). Princeton/Oxford, Princeton University Press.
Shore A. F. 1987. 'Egyptian Cartography', in J. B. Harley and D. Woodward (eds.), *The History of Cartography*, vol. 1. Chicago/London, University of Chicago Press: 117–29.
Sidebotham S. S., Hense M. and Nouwens H. M. 2008. *The Red Land: The Illustrated Archaeology of Egypt's Eastern Desert*. Cairo/New York, The American University in Cairo Press.

Tallet P. 2017. *Les papyrus de la mer Rouge I. Le journal de Merer. Papysur Jarf A et B*. Mémoires publiés par les membres de l'Institut français d'archéologie orientale 136. Cairo, Institut français d'archéologie orientale.
Te Velde H. 1967. *Seth, God of Confusion*. Leiden, Brill.
Trigger B. G., Kemp B. J., O'Connor D. and Lloyd A. B. 1983. *Ancient Egypt: A Social History*. Cambridge, Cambridge University Press.
van Pelt W. Paul 2013. 'Revising Egypto-Nubian Relations in New Kingdom Lower Nubia: From Egyptiannization to Cultural Entanglement', *Cambridge Archaeological Journal* 23.3: 523–50.
Ward C. A. 2000. *Sacred and Secular: Ancient Egyptian Ships and Boats*, AIA Monographs New Series, no. 5. Philadelphia, Archaeological Institute of America.
Weeks K. R. 2016. 'The Component Parts of KV Royal Tombs', in R. H. Wilkinson and K. R. Weeks (eds.), *The Oxford Handbook of the Valley of the Kings*. Oxford, Oxford University Press: 98–116.
Wilkinson R. H. 2000. *The Complete Temples of Ancient Egypt*. London, Thames and Hudson.
Wilkinson T. A. H. 1999. *Early Dynastic Egypt*. London, Routledge.
Willems H., Creylman H., De Laet V. and Verstraeten G. 2017. 'The Analysis of Historical Maps as an Avenue to the Interpretation of Pre-industrial Irrigation Practices in Egypt', in H. Willems and J.-M. Dahms (eds.), *The Nile: Natural and Cultural Landscape in Egypt: Proceedings of the International Symposium held at the Johannes Gutenberg-Universität Mainz, 22 & 23 February 2013*, Bielefeld, transcript Verlag: 255–346.
Wilson A. T. 1939. *The Suez Canal: Its Past, Present, and Future*. London/New York/Toronto, Oxford University Press.

3 Ancient Greece

> Past the Pillars of Herakles are many trading towns of the Carthaginians (...). In Europe the first people are the Iberes, a community of Iberia, with the river Iber. And two islands come next here, which have the name Gadeira. One of these two has a city that is a day's voyage distant from the Pillars of Herakles. Then a trading town and city, which has the name of Emporion, a Hellenic city; and these people are colonists from the Massaliotai. Coastal voyage of Iberia: seven days and seven nights.
>
> (Ps.-Scyl. 1–2)

Size and identity

Tiles of a mosaic

As for Egypt, a look at Google Earth immediately provides a starting point for the discussion (Figure 3.1): the core of the Greek galaxy consisted of a rugged land outlined by a variegated coast, and of over 1,200 islands located at a short distance from one another, all lapped by a relatively amicable sea (cf. Broodbank 2013: 76; Costantakopoulou 2007). According to the CIA's *World Factbook*, in the classification of the longest shorelines modern Greece occupies the eleventh position and is, at the same time, the smallest among the first sixteen countries of this list. All those kilometres of coasts are coiled up in a very small area, around a continental territory mainly made of mountains and hills, interspersed with patches of arable land (cf. Osborne 1987: 27–9; see also Van der Heyden and Scullard 1963: 12–7).

Already from the V millennium BCE the Greek world was inhabited by a mosaic of cultures and languages (Morkot 1996: 22). The II millennium BCE saw the rise of the Minoan and the Mycenaean civilisations, which traded extensively with southern Italian and Middle Eastern coasts, from where their goods reached Mesopotamia and Sudan. After their extinction,

DOI: 10.4324/9781003255314-4

Ancient Greece 55

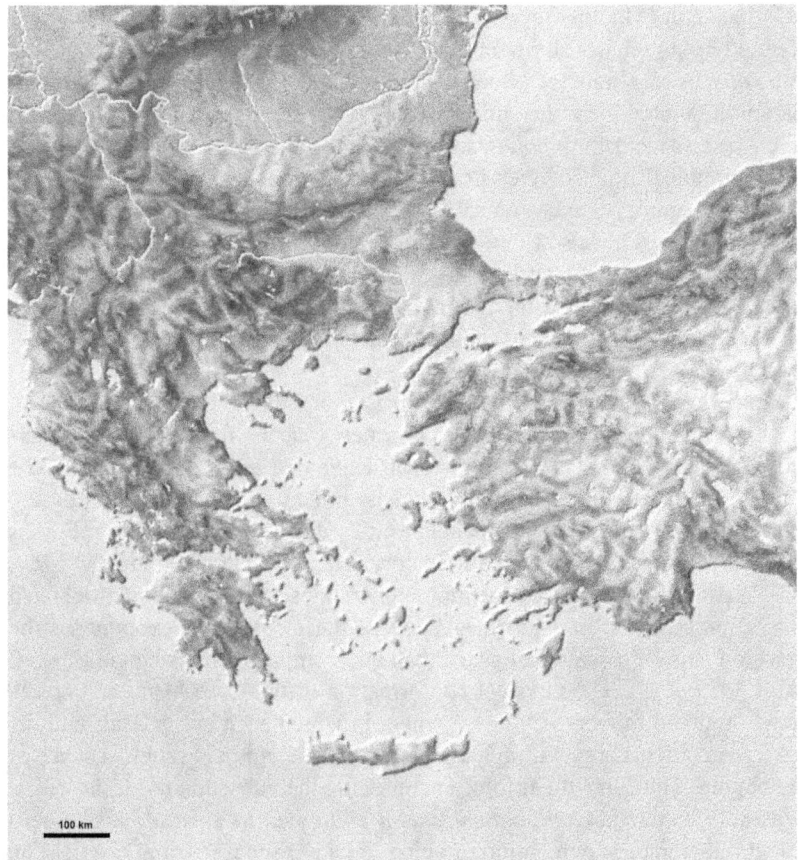

Figure 3.1 Physical map of Greece, from Google Earth.

perhaps triggered by a significant climate change (Drake 2012), from the XII to about the IX century BCE Greece went through a so-called 'dark age' (Hall 2014; Dickinson 2006), during which writing, sizeable towns and extensive trade, which had been typical of the Mycenean period, were completely absent. Archaeological evidence indicated a sharp rise in the population in the VIII century BCE, that, in turn, required and allowed a better exploitation of the arable land and encouraged the formation of larger settlements (Snodgrass 1980: chapter 1).

The original tribal system that characterised the earliest occupation of Greece survived well into the later periods, under the label *ethnos*: this word originally indicated a scattered population with common origins and shared religious cult (MacInerney 2001). It later took a slightly different meaning, defined by its relationship with the distinctive element of classical Greece: the *polis*, or city-state (cf. Morgan 2003). The VIII-century wave of urbanisation did not concern the entire Greek territory, and the birth of city-states even less so, and thus *poleis* and *ethne* did not necessarily overlap from a geographical point of view: the former developed all along the Aegean coasts, including Greece, Asia Minor, and all the islands in-between, but not in western Greece, where the latter remained predominant (Snodgrass 1980: 42–5; see also Hansen 2000b: 14–5). *Poleis* and *ethne* continued to exist in parallel (cf. Hutton 2005: 71–2), basically representing two ways of occupying a territory: concentrated into small entities and extended over vast areas.

Early *poleis* often consisted of clusters of villages converging around a single citadel. The adoption of this new, successful model of (apparently) independent settlement has been explained as a combination of the old Mycenean tradition of royal citadels, mixed with or overruled by the near-eastern example of independent cities devoted to the same religious cults and endowed with a small territory (Hansen 2000b; Snodgrass 1980: 31–2). To this one may add the more general observation that an articulated and compartmentalised territory, such as the Greek one, encouraged the development of a scatter of articulated and compartmentalised entities (cf. Ault 2019: 152). The physical conformation of the Greek land and coasts suggested and mirrored an arrangement in which each entity dealt with its own (catchment) area within a broader, cultural, and geographical sense of belonging. The centrifugal force encouraging the individuality of the *poleis* was only apparently predominant, as it continued to exist alongside centripetal factors: the perception of being linked to specific tribal origins (the *ethnos* in the ancient sense), the interdependence that characterised towns and villages, and, for both *poleis* and *ethne*, the fact of sharing the same environment and the same way of life.

The VIII-century sharp rise of the Greek population resulted in the progressive formation of a dense scatter of settlements that eventually amounted to about 800 *poleis* and about 700 colonies, that, in various historical periods and with alternating fortune, punctuated the Aegean and the coasts of Asia Minor, southern Italy, and the Black Sea (Figures 3.2 and 3.3; Hansen 2000a: 141 and 145; Whitley 2001: chapter 8; Hansen and Nielsen 2004; Ault 2019). As Osborne (1987: 24) wrote, 'as the same settlements increase in size, greater division of labour becomes possible and, more important, political change becomes almost mandatory'. The (re)introduction of an alphabet, this time inspired by the Phoenicians with the crucial addition of vowels (Freeman 1996: 65 and 86; Osborne 1987: 78–84), allowed a first codification of some laws (Whitley 2001: 188–90).

The various possible forms of government of a *polis* were described, with some differences, by Plato and Aristoteles, and included monarchy and tyranny (the oldest), aristocracy, oligarchy, timocracy, and democracy (Pl., *Resp.* 8.547c; Ober 1996; Davies 1993). Among them, Plato favoured aristocracy, whereas Aristoteles opted for timocracy ('a constitution based on a property classification', Arist., *Eth. Nic.* 1160a). In order to describe the government of *poleis*, we use the word 'democracy', but it must be underlined that Athenian democracy mainly concerned free male adult citizens; the number of rights enjoyed by the population declined when moving to women, and plummeted when reaching foreigners and slaves (Cohen 2000: chapter 6).

The marked individualism of the city-states represented their strength and their weak point: perennially engaged in competing against one another, they cultivated their own specific characteristics and, at the same time, implemented a similar agenda in the Mediterranean. The construction of the Greek identity and its relationship with seafaring is well summarised by Thucydides, writing on the Peloponnesian Wars:

> before the Trojan war there is no indication of any common action in Hellas, nor indeed of the universal prevalence of the name. (...) Indeed, they could not unite for this expedition till they had gained increased familiarity with the sea.
>
> (Thuc. 1.13)

How the sea lay at the centre of the Greek world is aptly summarised by Plato:

> I am convinced, then, that in the first place, if the Earth is round and (...) secondly (...) I believe that the Earth is very large and that we who dwell between the pillars of Hercules and the river Phasis [in modern Georgia] live in a small part of it about the sea, like ants or frogs about a pond, and that many other people live in many other such regions.
>
> (Pl., *Phd.* 108e–109b)

The image of the Mediterranean as a pond around which ants and frogs live is very effective. First of all, it conveys the impression of how the ancient communities busied themselves along the coasts of a relatively small sea. And then because it acts as a reminder: the pond might appear simple to handle to us... (modern scholars looking at the past from a comfortable

58 *Ancient Greece*

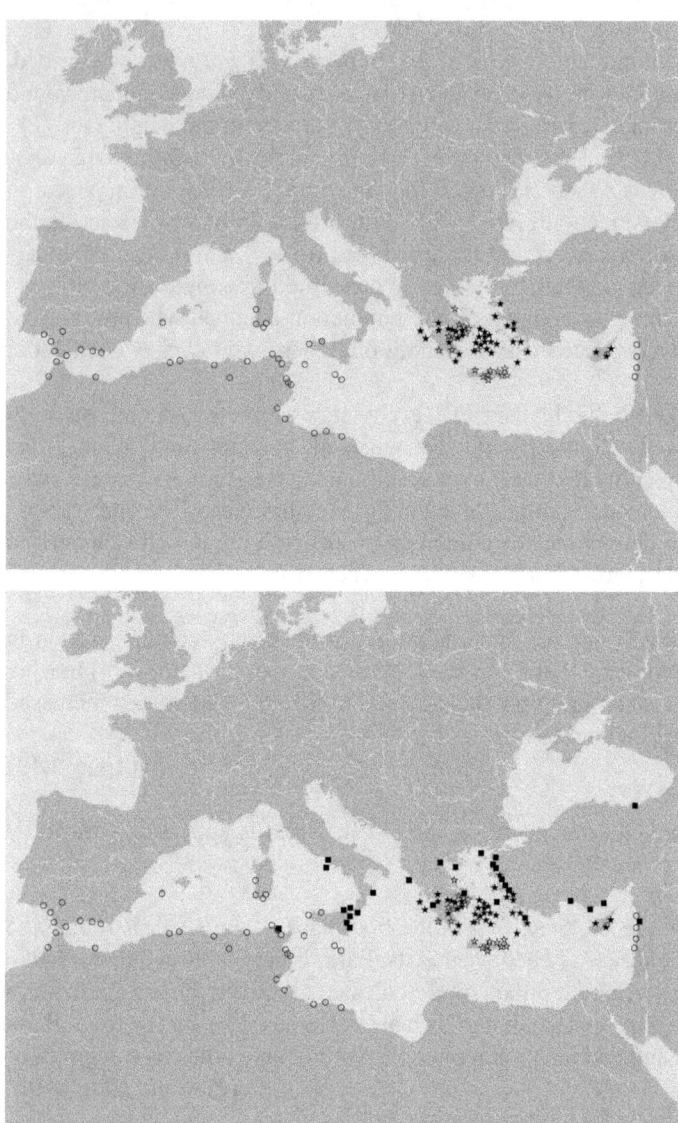

Figure 3.2a Phoenicial cities (empty circles) and progressive expansion of Greek cities: II millennium (empty stars), I millennium (stars) and VIII century BCE (squares).

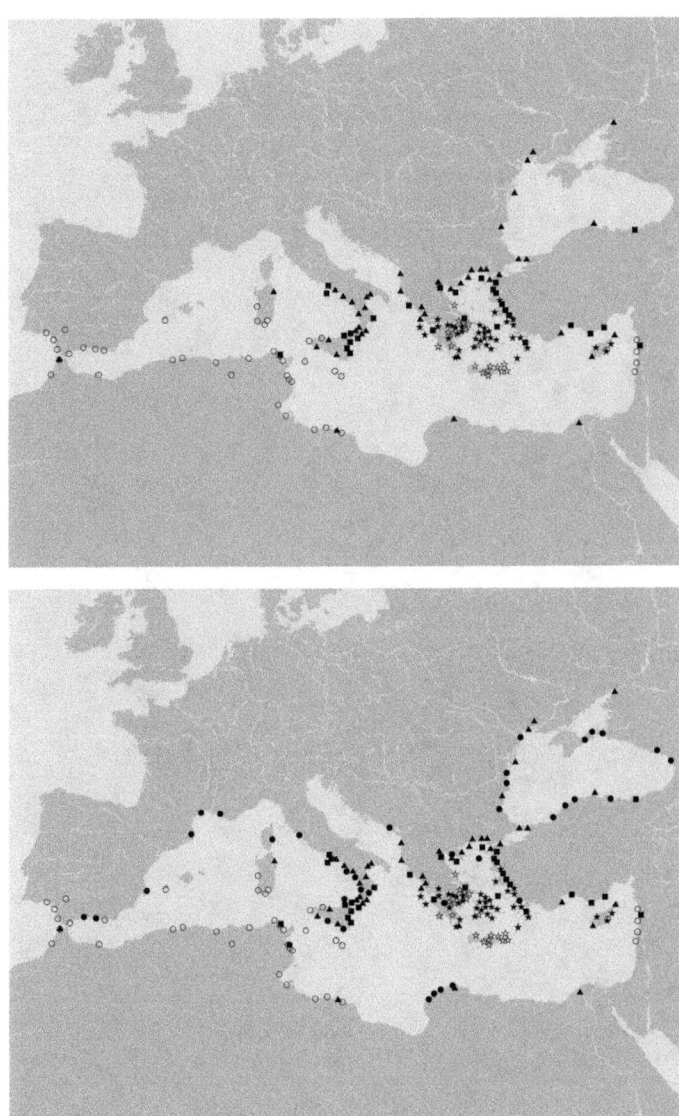

Figure 3.2b (Continued) VII century (triangles), VI century (circles), V century (vertical losanges) and IV century BCE (horizontal losanges).

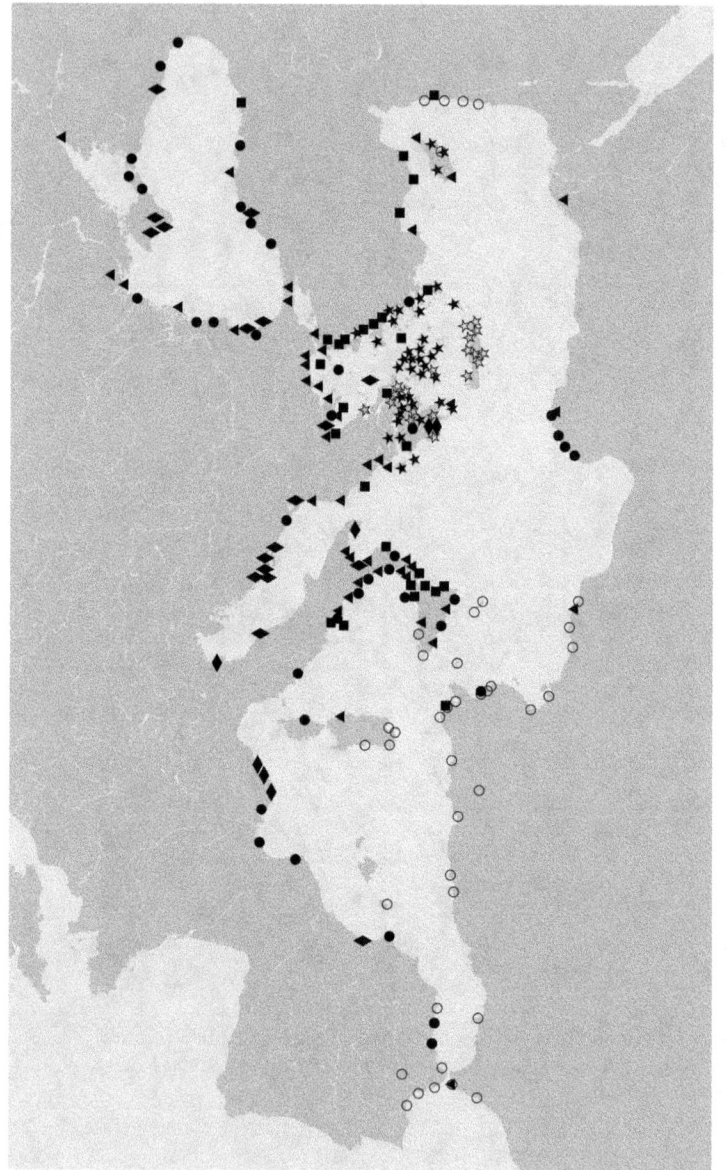

Figure 3.3 Combined view of Phoenician cities, Greek cities and their colonies from the II millennium to the IV century AD.

position) but, from the point of view of the ant or the frog, the pond poses a number of risks and dangers that can only be properly appreciated from their own point of view.

As we shall see below, the Greek city-states gave life to a peculiar way to expand their own individual interests and, at the same time, their common identity: they established a dense network of relations across the Aegean and Ionian seas, cast their net over the Mediterranean coasts, and attempted to spread even further, always moving by sea and always maintaining their original size, as an enduring impression of the territory that shaped them. As Malkin summarised, 'by the end of the Archaic period, the result of such processes was an overarching Hellenic network where physical space and the space of the collective imagination converged' (Malkin 2011: 12).

Size and effectiveness

We tend to make a distinction between cities, towns, villages, and countryside, but the ancient Greeks did not: the word *polis* referred to a unit made of settlement(s) and relating territory, bound together into a single entity within which the life of the community developed. Private properties of wealthy people, for instance, included goods in town, as well as land and food supply in the countryside; the surplus of the latter was sold and used to acquire luxury items and other goods. Athens, for instance, encompassed 139 village units spread over the territory of Attica (Osborne 1987: 11, 16–23, 63, 193–4).

The Greeks used the term *polis* to refer to the settlement and the social structure of the community that lived there, united by culture, traditions, religion, and symbols, as well as, sometimes, common origins (Hansen 1998: 17–20): 'every *polis* is (…) a sort of partnership (*koinonia*), and every partnership is formed with a view to some good' (Arist., *Pol.* 1.1252a). The term 'city-state' comes from the German *Stadtstaat*, coined in the mid-XIX century from the Roman concept of *civitas*, and only later transferred to the study of the Greek realm (Hansen 1994).

By our standards, city-states were small communities; in the ancient perception they *had* to be small. It is worth reading the reasons according to Aristoteles:

> Most people imagine that the prosperous *polis* must be a great state; but granted the truth of this, they fail to realize in what quality the greatness or smallness of a *polis* consists: they judge a great *polis* by the numerical magnitude of the population, but really the more proper thing to look at is not numbers but efficiency. For a *polis*, like other

things, has a certain function to perform. (...) There is a due measure of magnitude for a city-state as there also is for all other things, such as animals, plants, tools; each of these, if too small or excessively large, will not possess its own proper efficiency, but in some cases will have entirely lost its true nature and in others will be in a defective condition: for instance, a ship a span long will not be a ship at all, nor will a ship a quarter of a mile long, and even when it reaches a certain size, in some cases smallness and in others excessive largeness will make it sail badly. Similarly a state consisting of too few people will not be self-sufficing (*autarkes*), which is an essential quality of a state, and one consisting of too many, though self-sufficing in the mere necessaries, will be so in the way in which a nation (*ethnos*) is, and not as a state (*polis*).

(Arist., *Pol.* 7.1326a)

The actual size of Greek *poleis* was not uniform: the smallest covered only 10 km², most of them had a territory between 100 and 200 km², only 10% covered over 500 km², and only thirteen surpassed 1,000 km² (Hansen and Nielsen 2004; Hansen 2000b: 17). Most *poleis* had a population of over 1,000 inhabitants, and there is evidence that the population surpassed 10,000 individuals only in twenty-four cases (Hansen 1997: 25–31).

Athens represented an exception, as it covered c. 2,500 km² and its total population reached at some point 300,000 units; in the IV century BCE it was so large that it regularly needed to import additional grain to feed its population (Osborne 1987: 99). Defining Athens has never been easy, not even for the Greeks themselves (Hutton 2005: chapter 1). Herodotos indiscriminately used the word *polis* to denote 'town', 'state', and 'country'; he referred to Athens as a *polis* but only in a political sense and also called it *ethnos*. Apart from anomalous Athens, the other *poleis* were all smaller, even if powerful: Sparta controlled an area that in total was larger than Athens but divided into *poleis*; the area of influence of Boiotia included over twenty *poleis*; the small island of Kea, only 130 km², was always divided into four *poleis* (Cohen 2000: chapter 1).

In general, a manageable size was perceived to represent a basic characteristic of a city-state: if too large, 'it will not be easy for it to possess constitutional government: for who will command its over-swollen multitude in war? Or who will serve as its herald, unless he has the lungs of a Stentor?' (Arist., *Pol.* 7.1326a–b). Being able to directly communicate with all the citizens at the same time was clearly a fundamental aspect of a *polis*: it was not a matter of just being seen, but of being actually heard. Stentor, whose name survives in the adjective for 'loud' in several languages of Greek and Latin origin (like the Italian *stentoreo* and the Spanish *estentóreo*, but also in the

English *stentorian*), was a herald of the Greek army during the Trojan war, who was said to be endowed with 'the voice of fifty other men' (Hom., *Il.* 5.764), but clearly there were physical limits to be acknowledged.

Control was clearly the key issue:

> the proper configuration of the country it is not difficult to state (though there are some points on which the advice of military experts also must be taken): on the one hand it should be difficult for enemies to invade and easy for the people themselves to march out from.
> (Arist., *Pol.* 7.1326b–1327a)

The (ideal) shape of the *poleis* reflected a (simplified) social organisation:

> Hippodamus, son of Euryphon, a Milesian, who invented the division of cities into blocks (...), was the first man not engaged in politics who attempted to speak on the subject of the best form of constitution. His system was for a city with a population of ten thousand, divided into three classes; for he made one class of artisans, one of farmers, and the third the class that fought for the state in war and was the armed class. He divided the land into three parts, one sacred, one public and one private: sacred land to supply the customary offerings to the gods, common land to provide the warrior class with food, and private land to be owned by the farmers.
> (Arist., *Pol.* 2.1267b)

The reality was, of course, more complex than this. Older settlements evolved over the time mainly by filling the available space and adding public buildings; the strict planning rules could be applied to newly founded settlement, but the archaeological evidence suggests that this did not necessarily happen in a literal way (Bintliff 2010: 22–6). At any rate, according to the ideal founding principles, the shape of the urban space was meant not only to inherently reflect but also to openly declare the social organisation of the community.

As for the self-sufficiency that is often mentioned as a basic characteristic of a *polis*, it refers to self-government, rather than to the economic aspect: many Greek *poleis* developed in the shade of larger and more powerful *poleis*; several of them belonged to a federation or, as in the case of some colonies, remained dependent from their mother-cities (Hansen 1998: 73–83; 2000b: 18–9; 2000c: 17). In conclusion, even if independent in terms of government, Greek *poleis* belonged to a large-scale network of interconnected and interdependent entities, centred in Greece and spread along the coasts of the Eastern Mediterranean.

A web of relations

The history of Greece from the VII to the IV century BCE depicts the dense and complex web of relations that existed among the *poleis*: they traded, quarrelled, forged alliances, supported, and/or tried to subdue one another in a continuously changing scenario (e.g. Vlassopoulos 2009: 13–14; Hansen 2000a: 170–1; Osborne 1987: chapter 7). Piracy was a constant feature of this picture, meant both as the random action of plundering and raiding and as an element of warfare, applied against the enemy of the moment (De Souza 1999: 15–42). Only on one occasion, did they manage to build a common front against a major threat: the Persian attempt to conquer Greece (Gruen 2011: chapters 1 and 2). They did so only temporarily, though, and kept their internal distinctions and individual contributions clearly defined.

While city-states laboriously built their identities in an area with a radius of 300 km (cf. Cohen 2000: chapter 3), to the east of the Mediterranean, in the space of a few years, the Persian Empire greatly expanded its territory and overflowed into Asia Minor and Egypt, reaching a total extent of over 5.5 million km^2 (Figure 3.4; Green 1996: 6–10). After swallowing the recalcitrant Ionian cities, it identified western Greece as its next target (De Souza 2012: 9–17). However, the constellation of city-states proved to be incredibly resilient: they repelled two attempts to conquer the region, one in 492–490 BCE and another ten years later. The reasons behind the conflict and the way the events unfolded were recounted by Herodotos, about thirty years later; his Greek-centric view shaped the perception of the events for the centuries to come (see Balcer 1989 for a re-assessment from the Persian point of view).

On both occasions the large Persian army, well-organised in terms of intelligence, diplomatic warfare, and meticulous planning, was defeated by numerically inferior forces, 'quarrelsome, amateurish, ill-organized, but spontaneously courageous and irrepressible' (Lazenby 1993: viii, 29–31), made of contingents sent by city-states that managed to overcome their irreconcilable differences and forge temporary alliances in front of the greater, impending danger of being deprived of their freedom. The struggle was also ideological: 'on one side, the towering, autocratic figure of the Great King; on the other, the voluntary and imperfect discipline of proudly independent citizens' (Green 1996: 3).

On the field, on both occasions the Persians were defeated by the Greek ability to better exploit their meandering territory made of a succession of small spaces, rather than vast plains where a large army could unleash all its potential. The battles of Marathon, Salamis, and Plataea represent a good example of the importance of taking into account the shape of the territory when studying history: Peter Green used to take his students to Marathon

Ancient Greece 65

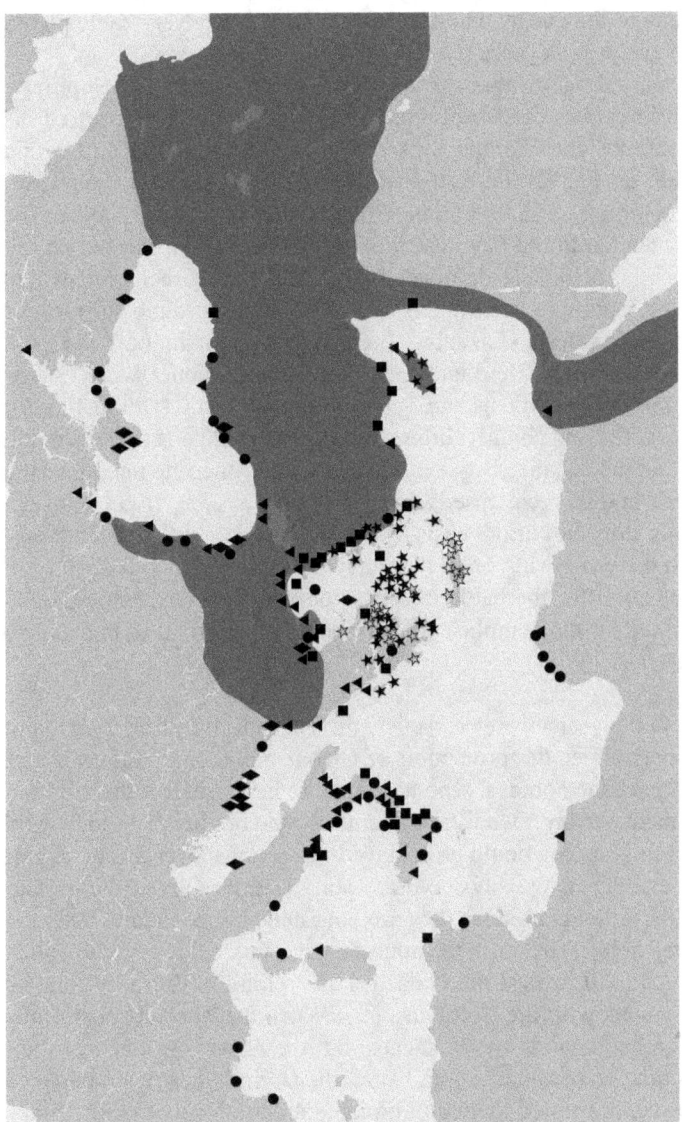

Figure 3.4 The western portion of the Persian Empire and the Greek *poleis*.

and lecture on the events on the spot, and discuss with colleagues possible interpretations of the events while walking around in the very same places where those events took place (Green 1996: xiii, see also xxvi).

Darius I started his conquest of the lands to the west of his empire by building a bridge over the Bosphorus, thanks to which he transferred his large army directly into Europe, crossed the Danube and invaded Scythia (Hartog 1988: chapter 2); he then sent towards Greece a vast contingent, probably amounting to 25,000 units (Green 1996: 12–3, 20–3). When the Persian fleet landed in the bay near the town of Marathon, located on the other side of the peninsula dominated by Athens, the Greeks intensified their contacts, thanks to messengers literally running around to transmit information and requests (Lazenby 1993: 33, 52–61). Among them, was Philippides, described by Herodotos as a long-distance runner, who covered the c. 150 km between Athens and Sparta in one day only (Hdt. 6.105–6); according to a later and slightly different tradition, a soldier, still covered in his armour, ran the distance between Marathon and Athens to announce the Greek victory, and then collapsed and died (Plut., *De glor. Ath.* 3 and Luc. *Laps.* 3). This story lies at the basis of the modern race called 'marathon', by definition the most tiring of all the running races.

The preparation for the battle of Marathon was a rather complex business, as testified by the complicated story behind the arrival of the contingent of Plataeans:

> When the Plataeans were pressed by the Thebans, they first tried to put themselves under the protection of Cleomenes son of Anaxandrides and the Lacedaemonians, who happened to be there. But they did not accept them, saying: 'we live too far away, and our help would be cold comfort to you. You could be enslaved many times over before any of us heard about it. We advise you to put yourselves under the protection of the Athenians, since they are your neighbours and not bad men at giving help'. The Lacedaemonians gave this advice not so much out of goodwill toward the Plataeans as wishing to cause trouble for the Athenians with the Boiotians. (…) When the Thebans heard this, they marched against the Plataeans, but the Athenians came to their aid. As they were about to join battle, the Corinthians, who happened to be there, prevented them and brought about a reconciliation. Since both sides desired them to arbitrate, they fixed the boundaries of the country (…). After rendering this decision, the Corinthians departed. The Boiotians attacked the Athenians as they were leaving but were defeated in battle. The Athenians went beyond the boundaries the Corinthians had made for the Plataeans, fixing the Asopus river as the boundary for the Thebans in the direction of Plataea and Hysiae. So

the Plataeans had put themselves under the protection of the Athenians in the aforesaid manner, and now came to help at Marathon.

(Hdt. 6.108)

Whatever happened behind the curtains, at the crucial moment and thanks to a brilliant tactical deployment of the available forces, the Greeks defeated the Persians, who decided to retreat.

Ten years later, Darius' son Xerxes launched a new, major invasion of the western portion of Greece; like his father, he also built a bridge to transfer his army, this time over the Hellespont. According to Herodotos, this time the (dis)proportion was 4,000 Greeks against three million Persians (Hdt 7.228); even if more realistic estimates fix the size of the invading army between 150,000 and 250,000 units, the disparity of forces and the heroism displayed by the Greeks remain impressively unchanged (Green 1996: 58–61; Lazenby 1993: 134–5). For three days, the small Greek contingent led by the Spartan king Leonidas blocked the passage to the large Persian army, until they were betrayed, attacked from the side through a mountain path and annihilated. And for three days in the waters of Artemision the assembled Greek fleet managed to resist the assault of the Persian fleet, which must have been at least three times larger (Lazenby 1993: chapter 6). When the Persians eventually flooded into Boiotia and then Attica, the population had already withdrawn to safety.

For the Greeks, this double defeat was a disaster in numerical terms, with half of their army killed and many ships damaged; but the heroism displayed by their soldiers and the perception of the Persian difficulties to organise the movements of their large army in Greece's narrow spaces represented a source of inspiration and encouragement. Even by combining the accounts of Herodotos, Aeschylus, Diodorus, and Plutarchos, it is unclear what happened next; the panic-stricken Greeks managed somehow to align themselves under the Athenian general Themistocles, who achieved a striking naval victory in the narrow waters near the island of Salamis, where the large Persian fleet was defeated in a ramming fight by the heavier and yet more agile Greek ships (Green 1996: 185–98).

The Greeks, as a whole, had won against the Persians; but the various *poleis* had a very clear idea of who did what. Herodotos reports that, at the battlefield of Thermopylai,

an inscription (…) reads as follows: 'Here four thousand from the Peloponnese once fought three million'. That inscription is for them all, but the Spartans have their own: 'Foreigner, go tell the Spartans that we lie here obedient to their commands'.

(Hdt 7.228)

In the following period, with the excuse of defending the region from the Persian Empire, Athens captained the creation of the Delian League, which soon turned into the occasion to brutally establish its supremacy. This Athenian 'empire' included all the islands and all the coasts around the Aegean Sea and cast its influence westwards in mainland Greece, while the powerful Sparta, securely nested in the mountainous region of Laconia, expanded its strictly military rule over most of the Peloponnesus. The conflict between these two city-states became inevitable: as recounted by Thucydides (Mynott 2013), the so-called Peloponnesian wars saw Athens and Sparta fighting against one another for twenty-seven years, either directly or by proxy, across the entire Aegean Sea, with the Persian Empire always dangerously looming in the background (for a summary De Souza 2012: 90–2).

A sweeping, unstoppable, and total conquest of Greece, Asia Minor and the entire Persian Empire did eventually take place: the author was Alexander the Great, and the enterprise started from Macedonia. The Macedonians had always been scorned by the Athenians: they were considered barbarians who had only recently ceased to be shepherds thanks to King Philip II, who had brought them down from the mountains and given them proper clothes and military training (cf. Arr., Anab. 7.9.2 as well as Demosthenes' lingering attitude in his Olynthiacs). During the V and IV centuries BCE, the Greek-speaking kingdom of Macedonia quietly absorbed lands rich in agricultural produce and mineral wealth to the north of the Aegean Sea. In 342–338, Philip crushed the resistance of Athens and Thebes in Greece and of Thrace to the east and was ready to launch a full-scale attack on Persia when he was killed.

His son Alexander took his place and started his epic expedition into the heart of the Persian Empire, that reached as far as India, and put together from scratch a huge empire stretching from southern Egypt to the feet of the Himalaya (Heckel and Tritle 2009). His sudden death in 323 BCE caused this large territory to be divided into vast regions: Egypt, unsurprisingly, quickly regained its usual territorial identity, whereas the subdivision of the Asian region was far less smooth and stable. Tiny Greece and Macedonia came into the sight of a new, emerging power: Rome, which absorbed them into a new, vast empire, again to be measured in millions of square kilometres, that diluted once and for all the Aegean quarrels (cf. Hansen 2000a: 149).

And yet, precise 'ethnic, linguistic and intermittently political divisions of ancient Greece' persisted: the II century CE traveller Pausanias divided his description of 'all Greek things' (not 'all of Greece') into ten books, each dedicated to a specific region, identified not only by its territory, but also by the origins of the local inhabitants (Hutton 2005: chapter 3, esp. 57 and 68–9). Blended as it was into the Roman Empire, the Greek galaxy proudly maintained the perception of its individual identities.

Travelling by sea

De-isolating

The Mediterranean is one of the few enclosed seas where navigation is relatively sheltered from the devastating hurricanes that sweep the oceans; and, among them, it is the only one lying in a mild climatic belt (Broodbank 2013: 61, Figure 2.2). The history of the communities stationed along its edges was deeply shaped by how they interacted with one another along communication routes that changed over time (cf. Rivers 2016). In the I millennium BCE, despite the difficulties, travelling by sea along sighting lines was easier than travelling by land. It was only with the Roman Empire that the latter received a significant impulse and spread to central Europe; however, crossing the Mediterranean by sea remained the quickest way to reach its shores.

The way in which ships were built until relatively recently meant that travelling at 90° to the wind was extremely difficult (Landels 2000: 141). For this reason, seafarers preferred to follow the coastline, exploiting the daily currents and winds, as well as having the possibility to quickly find shelter in case of need. The alternative was crossing vast expanses of sea: the advantage of more regular winds and of the absence of tides was countered by the danger of incurring storms or calms, by the necessity to be prepared to spend a long time at sea without fresh supplies and, especially, by the absence of sighting points.

The Mediterranean, although relatively small, does have a few 'blank' areas, corresponding to days and days of navigation without reference points. Its variegated coasts and large number of islands, especially in the eastern part, offered instead plenty of friendly waters to sail from landmark to landmark (Morton 2001; Horden and Purcell 2000: 123–43). Following Thiering (2012), one may observe that this environment encouraged the creation and adoption of mental models or, more specifically, cognitive maps of the surroundings which constituted the implicit knowledge laying at the basis of a commonsensical geographical experience. It is interesting that Homer did not distinguish between islands and peninsulas (Costantakopoulou 2007: 11, 20–8), thus giving more prominence to the movements across the watery areas than to the shape of the solid ground.

In terms of connectivity, islands have a special advantage: rather than being perceived as remote spots, isolated from the mainland, in a world made of ideally calm waters and populated by able seafarers, they are open on all sides to the possibility of being reached and could thus play an important role in the transmission of goods, people, and information (Horden and Purcell 2000: 224–30; see also Malkin 2011: 207–9). In several European languages an 'island' is automatically 'isolated': Greek islands, however, far from being isolated lands in the middle of an ocean, lie at a short distance from one another, and could thus be exploited in terms of both isolation and connectivity (Chiai 2012; Costantakopoulou 2007: 3–5).

Groups of islands close to one another could even function as single units, in which the various elements played different roles; one case is the long-lasting habit to reserve some tiny islands, difficult to exploit for agricultural purposes, to herds of goats, able to survive for long periods drinking salty water (Costantakopoulou 2007: chapter 6, esp. 200–14). These groups of islands could function as 'exploded' communities, in which the frequency and intensity of the mutual contacts depended on their mutual distances (e.g. Broodbank 2013: 307–8). Travelling from one to another might be considered relatively easy, but experimental reconstructions of the navigation conditions remind us that this was not necessarily the case: the picture, published by Broodbank (2013: 153), of five half-naked men roaming on a hypothetical reed boat from Attica to Melos via the chain of islands of Kea, Kythnos, Seriphos, and Siphnos represents yet another occasion to grasp, in one single image, all the difficulties of the earliest journeys across what we now define an 'amicable' sea.

The construction of boats and ships evolved rapidly, especially in terms of the shape of the hull, and of methods to join their components and steering systems (Landels 2000: 135 ff. and appendix): by the V century BCE the Mediterranean was crossed by fast and agile triremes, ships propelled by sails and three lines of rowers (Morrison, Coates, and Rankov 2000; see also Thuc. 1.14). The largest were 40 m long and 6 m wide. As in most ships of all periods, space was extremely limited: rowers were placed at a horizontal distance of c. 80 cm from one another, and directly below the bottoms of the rower of the upper line (cf. the crude remarks in Aristophanes' *Frogs*; Ar. *Ran.* 1074), and within this space they had to rhythmically row and, in general, spend their time at sea (cf. Landels 2000: appendix).

The evolution of the fleets meant the construction of a network of medium- and long-range connections among maritime basins, in turn linked to major routes along which people moved on land (Costantakopoulou 2007: 222–6). The coasts and waters of the eastern portion of the Mediterranean remained easier to navigate and to keep under control in comparison with the western portion: moving westwards, the Greek familiarity with the sea and the land progressively diminished (Broodbank 2013: 417) and found its physical and mental boundary in the Pillars of Herakles, the modern Strait of Gibraltar (Pind., *Ol.* 3).

Periploi

Travelling by sea consisted of moving, preferably along the coast, from harbour to harbour, where ships could shelter and refill their supplies – provided, of course, that the mutual relations were good. The Athenian ships approaching southern Italy during the ill-planned attempt to subdue Sicily (e.g. Smith 2004), for instance, did not meet a particularly warm welcome:

> The whole fleet now struck across the Ionian sea from Corcyra. They arrived at the promontory of Iapygia and at Tarentum, each ship taking its own course, and passed along the coast of Italy. The Italian cities did not admit them within their walls, or open a market to them, but allowed them water and anchorage; Tarentum and Locri refused even these. At length they reached Rhegium, the extreme point of Italy, where the fleet reunited.
>
> (Thuc. 6.44.1–2)

Moving from place to place along the coast thus represented the standard way of travelling by sea. *Periploi* were documents that listed, in order, the ports and coastal landmarks, providing approximate intervening distances, that a vessel could expect to find along a shore (Dueck 2012: 51–60). A product of the ancient Mediterranean coastal seafaring, they were clearly based on the direct experience of seafarers (cf. Thiering 2012), but were not an organic corpus of documents, and did not all have the same purpose.

One of the earliest *periploi* dates to the VI century BCE and describes a commercial journey made by a Greek, whose name has not survived, who travelled from Massalia (modern Marseille) to Tartessos, located somewhere in southern Spain (Dueck 2012: 52). The *periplous* of Pseudo-Scylax, written around 338–337 BCE, instead describes the coasts of the Mediterranean and the Black Sea, starting from Gibraltar, moving clockwise, and eventually returning to the starting point (Figure 3.5). Important information can be extracted from the analysis of this text: it does not seem to be a seafarer guide, although it does contain information that would be useful to navigate. In particular, it provides distances both in days and in *stadia*, a Greek unit of measurement that was not standardised until the Ptolemaic and Roman periods; navigation times were probably far more useful in practical terms, as seafaring took place without the aid of measuring instruments. The author probably drew information from different sources, written and oral, and linked it together into a sequential description of the most important itineraries that unravelled along the coasts of the known world (Shipley 2011).

The *periplous* of Pseudo-Scylax:

> is not intended to convey an over-arching concept of 'the Mediterranean' as such; it gives the sea no name, and additionally covers the Black Sea and part of Atlantic Morocco. It is not simply a picture of the world

72 *Ancient Greece*

Figure 3.5 Coastal maritime routes according to the *periplous* of Pseudo-Scylax (thicker line), with connectivity among Aegean islands highlighted (broken lines).

where Greeks have settled, for it covers NW Africa to the west of Cyrenaica, where there were no Greek cities, and includes 'barbarian' regions like Phoenicia. Since, however, he repeatedly expressed a distinction between Hellenic and barbarian communities, the author may be trying, consciously or subconsciously, to define the extent of the world, and the relationships between its parts, in terms of its potential to be visited, exploited, or ultimately controlled by the Greeks. Perhaps he intended to bring into a single frame the whole of 'the world that we can access'. (...) His work is, in short, a work of geography.

(Shipley 2011: 13)

Such a document describes an appropriation of the space taken along paths which were experienced by travellers and not necessarily transposed into abstract maps. Moving from place to place can be found again in Pausanias' description of Greece, dating to the II century CE (400 years later). Here the sea journey to Greece is described 'for one sailing past the cape ...', 'for one sailing onwards ...' and is followed by one on land, moving from place to place: the text appears to describe an itinerary, along which places and monuments are described as laying 'near', 'not far', or 'beyond' (Hutton 2005: 13–4). The description of the journey is here based on the intersection between what the author saw (the physical landscape) and what he knew and expected (his cognitive landscape), merged into a cognitive mapping process (Hutton 2005: 54). It thus combines the physical aspect and an interpretation of the surrounding world: from the latter depend both the choice of what should be included and how it should be described, as well as the attempt to fill the gaps and try to imagine what lies beyond.

The fact that the word referring to a 'geographical representation' used by both Herodotos and Aristophanes is *periodos* (lit. 'way around', cf. Clarke 1999: 9) confirms that the progressive knowledge of the space depended on the progressive acquaintance with a sequence of places.

Lines of knowledge

The way in which people moved around shaped their knowledge of the surrounding world. This is mirrored by the Greek perception of the world in the archaic age, as filtered by the Homeric poems and Hesiod, as that of a central core centred around the Mediterranean and bordered by the 'river Ocean' that surrounded everything and stretched to an unimaginable distance (Dueck 2012: 23–3; Geus 2018).

The core of the world was the *oikoumene*, the inhabited land, as opposed to empty and desert areas (Dueck 2012: 4–5). Sailing beyond the known world could be a terrifying experience: Herodotos reports that Sataspes, sent by the Persian king Xerses on an expedition beyond the Pillars of Herakles, 'sailed south; but when he had been many months sailing over the sea, and always more before him, he turned back and made sail for Egypt' (Hdt 4.43). The natural fear of the unknown combined with the strict control that the Carthaginians held over the Western Mediterranean, aided by exaggerated tales of the perils awaiting sailors beyond, meant to discourage and prevent the Greeks from gaining knowledge and familiarity with that area. As a consequence, for a long time the Pillars of Herakles represented a forbidding *non plus ultra*, a warning to mariners not to proceed any further; this lasting impression continued even after the Phoenician influence had ceased (Casson 1994: 59–60; Romm 1992: 17–9).

When describing the world, Herodotos focused on what was actually known, and could be proved: 'the opinion about Ocean is grounded in obscurity and needs no disproof; for I know of no Ocean river; and I suppose that Homer or some older poet invented this name and brought it into his poetry' (Hdt 2.23; see also Hdt. 4.8). He tended to describe the known world as made of symmetric entities (cf. Thomas 2000: 77–8), but also acknowledged the existence of unseen territories and empty spaces:

> If there are men beyond the north wind, then there are others beyond the south. And I laugh to see how many have before now drawn maps of the world, not one of them reasonably; for they draw the world as round as if fashioned by compasses, encircled by the Ocean river, and Asia and Europe of a like extent. For myself, I will in a few words indicate the extent of the two, and how each should be drawn.
>
> (Hdt. 4.36)

No ancient Greek map survives; Strabo wrote that Anaximander 'was the first to publish a geographical board' (*geographikon pinaka*, Str. 1.1.11), and we know that maps were exposed under porticos in III century BCE Athens, but we can only guess what they looked like (Harley, Woodward, and Aujac 1987a: 134–5 and 1987b: 158).

Herodotos reported the existence of areas where the environmental conditions do not encourage or allow humans and animals to live (Hdt. 3.98 and 4.185). Apart from physical limitations, it is clear that for him the real limits are those of his knowledge, not necessarily of the Earth: speaking about the populations stationed in the northern region of the *oikoumene*, he wrote that 'I know and can tell the names of all the peoples that live on the ridge as far as the Atlantes, but no farther than that' (Hdt. 4.185, see also 4.17).

Concerning the nature of the edges of the known world, if the earliest descriptions referred to a definite area clearly surrounded by a watery entity, progressively they moved from being hypothetical physical limits to corresponding to progressively changing limits of an evolving knowledge. This geographical knowledge grew by accretion mainly along communication routes that may be extended or opened for commercial and/or military reasons (Geus 2003). Moving across the world (be it known or unknown) was carried out always in the same way: step by step, along known directions or at least following the same rules, and trying to avoid the adverse elements.

Dots and lines

So near, and yet so far

The Homeric poems depict, in the background, just the world that has been described so far: the *Ilias*, set in the final weeks of the 10-year long siege of Troy, tells how the various Greek contingents managed to find a common line of intervention among their usual and perpetual bickering; and the *Odysseia* tells us how difficult it was for Odysseus, after the war against Troy, to sail back to his homeland, the island of Ithaca, located at a distance of 'only' 500 km as the crow flies. A relatively easy journey – if one only knew where to go and had the gods on his side.

The journey back home proceeded relatively smoothly at the beginning, but soon Odysseus and his men were caught by a fierce gale:

> Zeus raised the North wind against us till it blew a blast of wind, so that land and sky were hidden in thick clouds, and night sprang forth out of the heavens. We let the ships run before the gale, but the force of the wind tore our sails to tatters, so we took them down for fear of shipwreck, and rowed our hardest towards the land. There we lay two days and two nights suffering much alike from toil and distress of mind, but on the morning of the third day we again raised our masts, set sail, and took our places, letting the wind and steersmen direct our ship. I should have got home at that time unharmed had not the north wind and the currents been against me as I was doubling Cape Malea, and set me off my course hard by the island of Cythera. I was driven thence by foul winds for a space of nine days upon the sea, but on the tenth day we reached the land of the Lotus-eaters.
>
> (Hom., *Od.* 9.2)

During their subsequent visit to the island where the Cyclops lived, Odysseus deceived, blinded and even taunted Polyphemus, a son of the god Poseidon, who, as a revenge, set a curse on him and his men. Odysseus then stopped at the island inhabited by the god of the winds, Aeolus, asked for his help but omitted to say that Poseidon was angry at him. Aeolus accepted to constrain all the adverse winds into a bag, and leave out only the western wind that would have taken Odysseus back home; as the latter recounts, however:

> it all came to nothing, for we were lost through our own folly. Nine days and nine nights did we sail, and on the tenth day our native land showed on the horizon. We got so close in that we could see the stubble fires burning, and I, being then dead tired, fell into a light sleep, for I had never let the rudder out of my own hands, that we might get home the faster. On this the men fell to talking among themselves, and said I was bringing back gold and silver in the sack that Aeolus had given me. (…) Thus they talked and evil counsels prevailed. They loosed the sack, whereupon the wind flew howling forth and raised a storm that carried us weeping out to sea and away from our own country. Then I awoke, and knew not whether to throw myself into the sea or to live on and make the best of it; but I bore it, covered myself up, and lay down in the ship, while the men lamented bitterly as the fierce winds bore our fleet back to the Aeolian island.
>
> (Hom., *Od.* 10.1)

There Aeolus, having discovered that he had been deceived, refused to help Odysseus and his men; opposed by sea, winds, and gods, they started an erratic journey across the Mediterranean that lasted for years. Since the earliest times, scholars have tried to reconstruct this journey and match it with precise locations, some with the aid of maps of the Mediterranean (Romm 1992: 183–96; Severin 1987; cf. Dueck 2012: 21–2). The difficulties of this enterprise, tarnished by the doubt that most of the destinations might be imaginary, are so significant that already Eratosthenes apparently said that 'you will find the scene of the wanderings of Odysseus when you find the cobbler who sewed up the bag of the winds' (Str. 1.2.15).

Whether or not the places visited by Odysseus were real, some specific details of his adventures certainly feel so: how the men spent the night during the first gale, and the moment in which they were so close to Ithaca to be able to see the fires burning are two vivid descriptions that clearly draw from the actual experience of real sailors, who could see their efforts blown away by hostile winds and waters.

Production and reproduction

Since the earliest times, the entire Greek history was characterised by continuous movements across Greece, Asia Minor, and the Western Mediterranean; some were determined by the forced displacement of populations, others by the precise will to establish new settlements elsewhere. Modern historiography tends to classify some of these movements as 'migrations' or 'invasions', thus conveying a different meaning in comparison with the more reassuring 'colonisation', that appears to imply a carefully planned strategy. Modern attempts to strictly classify the ancient Greek movements are 'a product of the interplay between ancient and modern ideologies of colonisation' (Wilson 2006: 25–31, esp. 26).

A good description of all these intertwined movements can be found in Strabo:

> The country had then come to be so populous, that the Athenians even sent forth a colony of Ionians to the Peloponnesus, and caused the country which they occupied to be called Ionia after themselves, instead of Aegialus; and the men were divided into twelve cities (...). But after the return of the Heracleidae they were driven out by the Achaeans and went back again to Athens; and from there they sent forth with the Codridae the Ionian colony to Asia, and these founded twelve cities on the seaboard of Caria and Lydia, thus dividing themselves into the same number of parts as the cities they had occupied in the Peloponnesus.
>
> (Str. 8.7.1)

Greek cities remained cities: their size and population varied within a relatively broad range, and yet they never physically and numerically grew over a certain limit. A modern version of the description by Aristoteles of the cities as organisms could be that the size of *poleis* was basically defined by their DNA; as we have seen, the only exception (up to a certain point) was Athens. Following the same metaphorical description, referring to the operation of establishing colonies, one might say that *poleis* reproduced themselves by cell division.

A colony could be defined as an *apoikia*, or as an *emporion*. *Apoikia* meant 'home away from home': these colonies were new communities in their own right, with their own territory and urban centre, their own citizens and laws. Every *apoikia* had a mother-city (*metropolis*), from which its founder and the majority of the inhabitants came; the two cities generally maintained good ties, and *apoikiai* could appeal to mother-cities for help in time of crisis. It is possible that the foundation of *apoikiai* was triggered by a demographic growth that the mother-city was unable to absorb, and/or the need for further agricultural land (Wilson 2006: 25–7). An *emporion* was instead a settlement devoted to facilitating trade between Greeks and 'barbarians'; *emporia* were not intended to be autonomous political communities, did not necessarily have a mother-city, and their inhabitants were diverse and more cosmopolitan.

Systematisations can help, but facts are often more complicated: the relationships among cities were not always simple and linear, and the often differing foundation myths suggest that a city's origins might be presented in different ways depending on the target audience (Mac Sweeney 2015, esp. chapter 2; Malkin 2011: chapter 4). At any rate, religion played a fundamental role and represented a unifying factor (Malkin 1987 and 2011: chapters 2 and 3; see also Rutherford 2009 on the movements of religious delegations). Sometimes initial distinctions faded away, as happened for instance with Naukratis, in Egypt, which started as an *emporion* and then basically became a *polis* (Whitley 2001: 124); and sometimes distinctions are just hard to make, as in the case of Pithekoussai (Wilson 2006: 34). In general, even if it is difficult to establish whether the main reason to establish a colony was related to trade or wealth (Whitley 2001: 125–7), establishing settlements at favourable positions was the Greek way to expand and reproduce. Citizens were linked to their communities and to their political character rather than to their physical territory, and thus people moved away from their original *polis* without losing their identity (Vegetti 1989: 47).

When Odysseus landed on an island near the land of the Cyclopes, he evaluated it from the point of view of a potential settler (cf. Wilson 2006: 39):

> For the isle is nowise poor, but would bear all things in season. In it are meadows by the shores of the grey sea, well-watered meadows and soft, where vines would never fail, and in it level ploughland, whence they might reap from season to season harvests exceeding deep, so rich is the soil beneath; and in it, too, is a harbour giving safe anchorage, where there is no need of moorings, either to throw out anchor-stones or to make fast stern cables, but one may beach one's ship and wait until the sailors' minds bid them put out, and the breezes blow fair. Now at the head of the harbour a spring of bright water flows forth from beneath a cave, and round about it poplars grow.
> (Hom., *Od.* 9.130–140)

Obviously, islands were ideal places to establish colonies, especially if new to the area: settling on an island would have guaranteed isolation and thus protection from whatever happened on the mainland (Costantakopoulou 2007: 7–8), as the case of the colonies established around modern Napoli, in southern Italy, clearly attest: from Pithekoussai on the island now called Ischia, Greek settlers later moved to the hilltops of two peninsulas, where they founded Cuma and Parthenope; the latter was later renamed Paleopolis ('old city') when Neapolis (the 'new city') was founded down in the plain (Whitley 2001: 114 and 126–7).

If all these settlements are represented by dots and their relations by lines indicating the flows, the ancient Greek world can be aptly represented as a decentralised network (Malkin 2011: 17–9). A constant of this world was the sea. As Horden and Purcell noted (2000: 27), the liberating shout '*thalassa, thalassa!*' ('sea, sea!') that, according to Xenophon, the Greek troops let out after wandering for months across the Anatolian mountains stood 'as a symbol of the attachment of many ancient people to a determinate Mediterranean world' (cf. also Dan 2012).

Step by step

As Horden and Purcell noted (2000: 24), the Greeks ruled over a network of communications. They entertained short-, medium-, and long-range affairs among themselves, depending on the scale of the movements that were necessary. *Poleis* fighting against one another within the relatively restricted area of the Ionian Sea moved within a relatively short radius; colonies, that is, the operation of extending the same pattern beyond their original geographical core, represented a successful way to extend the Greek presence beyond the original geographical core. Phoenicians and Carthaginians had been moving along and across the Mediterranean in a similar way.

This colonial system, made of points connected by maritime lines, had the potential to expand as long as the same pattern could be replicated. By the VI century BCE, the major powers along the Mediterranean coasts had gathered enough experience and information to attempt long-distance expeditions. The method adopted to increase their range was a variation of the usual system: proceeding by steps, joining together sequences of relatively short segments, this time in a precise direction but towards an unknown destination.

Between the VI and the V centuries BCE, Carthage sent two expeditions beyond the Pillars of Herakles, with two different purposes: one led by Himlico, heading north, which perhaps reached south-western Britain (Dueck 2012: 54–5), and one led by Hanno, heading south. The latter was an incredibly ambitious enterprise, to the point that some scholars believe that the texts do not describe a real journey (Jacob 1991: 84). Hanno's expedition was said to consist of about 30,000 men and women, loaded on sixty fifty-oared ships, that travelled beyond the Pillars of Herakles and continued south along the African coast. Its scope was to progressively extend the Carthaginian influence thanks to the creation of colonies, thus replicating the scheme which had been successfully adopted within the Mediterranean. Therefore, from time to time, groups of people were dropped ashore to found new cities in favourable positions. As their southbound journey progressed, the travellers met with increasingly difficult conditions and more hostile populations. The rather scant written description does not allow to establish exactly how far they went: the lowest estimate is Sierra Leone, the highest Cameroon or Gabon; in any case, a formidable enterprise (Cartwright 2016). No traces survive of the colonies founded along the route.

Other long-range expeditions had a more exploratory character. Although the possibility of eventually establishing new commercial routes is likely to have been a major trigger of all these enterprises, expeditions that headed beyond the known world had a less defined and predictable outcome. Travellers became explorers and collected information and experiences which were alien to the Mediterranean world.

Between the end of the VII and the beginning of the VI century BCE, the Egyptian pharaoh Necho II sent an expedition to prove that Libya (modern Africa) could be circumnavigated. Herodotos reports that:

> When he had finished digging the canal which leads from the Nile to the Arabian Gulf, he sent Phoenicians in ships, instructing them to sail on their return voyage past the Pillars of Herakles until they came into the northern sea and so to Egypt. So the Phoenicians set out from the Red Sea and sailed the southern sea; whenever autumn came they would put in and plant the land in whatever part of Libya they had reached, and there await the harvest; then, having gathered the crop, they sailed on, so that after two years had passed, it was in the third that they rounded the pillars of Herakles and came to Egypt.
>
> (Hdt. 4.42)

Differently from Hanno's expedition, in this case the same group of travellers completed the journey by settling and then moving away from favourable places along the coast. They followed the system normally adopted to establish colonies along the coasts, but in this case the settlements were only meant to be temporary camps, to be soon dismissed to move on to a new destination.

Even if the journey followed a familiar pattern, the explorers encountered places and phenomena that were unknown to them: 'they said (what some may believe, though I do not) that in sailing around Libya they had the sun on their right hand' (Hdt. 4.42). This final remark by Herodotos offers a clue suggesting that the expedition might have been indeed successful: while sailing westwards beyond the Cape of Good Hope, the sun of the southern hemisphere would have appeared to the right of the sailors.

Some situations were just too different from the usual environmental conditions to which Mediterranean sailors were used to to be properly described: when the Greek geographer Pytheas circumnavigated Britain in the years 310–306 BCE, he described an uninhabitable world,

Ancient Greece 81

where land properly speaking no longer exists, nor sea nor air, but a mixture of these things, like a 'marine lung', in which it is said that earth and water and all things are in suspension as if this something was a link between all these elements, on which one can neither walk nor sail.

(Str. 2.4.1)

This phenomenon has been tentatively identified with the presence of frozen fog and drifting ice, conditions indeed quite different from those to which Mediterranean sailors were used.

In conclusion, Phoenicians, Carthaginians, and Greeks all physically moved along the Mediterranean coasts in a very similar way, dictated by the ancient navigation methods. While in the first and second case the system of dots and maritime lines irradiated from specific areas (Carthage and the area identified as Phoenicia), in the third case this was the very structure of Greek civilisation, born itself on an interconnected network of islands. Greek *apoikiai* were far more similar to their mother-cities than Phoenician and Carthaginian colonies, generally much smaller and far more influenced by the indigenous culture of the area where they were founded (Sommer 2009).

The environment in which the Greeks successfully moved to 'colonise' (in a wide and non-committal sense of the word) the world step by step by spreading their network consisting of dots and lines corresponded to the Mediterranean type of coasts. As Malkin noted, 'the Greeks called the Mediterranean and the Black Sea *he hemetera thalassa* ("our sea"), but did so only in a metaphorical sense'. The Romans also called the Mediterranean *Mare Nostrum*, but in a different way:

> Instead of Greeks looking 'inside', from their nodes on the shores towards the shared sea, the Romans observed it from the centre (Rome) outward, towards the coasts. (…) Links, both planned and random, rapidly reduced the distance between the nodes of the network, turning the vast Mediterranean and the Black Sea into a 'small world' (…). These networks informed, sometimes created, and even came to express what we call Greek civilization.

(Malkin 2011: 4–5)

As for Egypt, the Greek model of appropriation of space may also be linked to environmental factors. Differently from Egypt, where this connection was deeply rooted to a specific, large, homogeneous, self-contained place, the Greeks replicated their pattern made of relatively small places whenever they could physically reach *another* suitable small place, that could be thus incorporated in a communication network. The leading factor of the spread of the Greek civilisation was therefore the connectivity among similar small places. The connections were mainly maritime, and the similitude concerned the possibility of establishing *polis*-like settlements. As we shall see in the following chapters, the Roman Empire expanded both aspects: an increased connectivity increased the assimilation of places.

Bibliographical references

Primary sources

Ar. *Ran.*: Aristophanes, *Ranae*.
Arist., *Eth. Nic.*: Aristoteles, *Ethica Nicomachea*.
Arist., *Pol.*: Aristoteles, *Politica*. English translation from the Perseus Digital Library (perseus.tufts.edu).
Arr., *Anab.*: *Arrian*, Anabasis.
Hdt.: Herodotus, *Historiae*. English translation from the Perseus Digital Library (perseus.tufts.edu).
Hom., *Il.*: Homer, *Iliad*. English translation from the Perseus Digital Library (perseus.tufts.edu).
Hom., *Od.*: Homer, *Odyssey*. English translation from the Perseus Digital Library (perseus.tufts.edu).
Luc. *Laps.*: Lucian, *Pro lapsu inter salutandum*.
Pl., *Phd.*: Plato, *Phaedo*. English translation from the Perseus Digital Library (perseus.tufts.edu).
Pl., *Resp.*: Plato, *Respublica*.
Plut., *De glor. Ath.*: Plutarchus, *De gloria Atheniensium*.
Ps.-Scyl.: Pseudo-Scylax, *Periplous*. English translation from Shipley G. 2011. *Pseudo-Skylax's Periplous. The Circumnavigation of the Inhabited World*. Exeter, Bristol Phoenix Press.
Pind., *Ol.*: Pindarus, *Olympian*.
Str.: Strabo, *Geographia*. English translation from the Perseus Digital Library (perseus.tufts.edu).
Thuc.: Thucydides, *History of the Peloponnesian War*. English translation from the Perseus Digital Library (perseus.tufts.edu).

Secondary sources

Ault B. A. 2019. 'Synoikismos: Formation and Form of Ancient Greek Cities', in A. Gyucha (ed.), *Coming Together: Comparative Approaches to Population Aggregation and Early Urbanization*. Albany, State University of New York Press: 149–61.
Balcer J. M. 1989. 'The Persian Wars against Greece: A Reassessment', *Historia: Zeitschrift für Alte Geschichte* 38.2: 127–43.
Bintliff J. L. 2010. 'Classical Greek Urbanism: A Social Darwinian View', in R. M. Rosen and I. Sluiter (eds.), *Valuing Others in Classical Antiquity*. Mnemosyne Supplement 323. Leiden/Boston, Brill.

Broodbank C. 2013. *The Making of the Middle Sea: A History of the Mediterranean from the Beginning to the Emergence of the Classical World*. London, Thames and Hudson.

Cartwright M. 2016. 'Hanno: Carthaginian Explorer', *Ancient History Encyclopedia*, Online Version (https://www.ancient.eu/article/913/hanno-carthaginian-explorer/, consulted in March 2018).

Casson L. 1994. *Travel in the Ancient World*. Baltimore/London, Johns Hopkins University Press.

Chiai G. F. 2012. 'Thinking Space: Insularity as Mental Model', in K. Geus and M. Thiering (eds.), *Common Sense Geography and Mental Modelling*. Berlin, Max Planck Institute for the History of Science, MPIWG Preprint 426: 45–56.

Clarke K. 1999. *Between Geography and History: Hellenistic Constructions of the Roman World*. Oxford Classical Monographs. Oxford, Clarendon Press.

Cohen E. E. 2000. *The Athenian Nation*. Princeton, Princeton University Press.

Costantakopoulou C. 2007. *The Dance of the Islands: Insularity, Networks, the Athenian Empire, and the Aegean World*. Oxford Classical Monographs. Oxford, Oxford University Press.

Dan A. 2012. 'Xenophon's *Anabasis* and the Common Greek Mental Modelling of Space', in K. Geus and M. Thiering (eds.), *Common Sense Geography and Mental Modelling*. Berlin, Max Planck Institute for the History of Science, MPIWG Preprint 426: 57–73.

Davies J. K. 1993. *Democracy and Classical Greece*. Cambridge, Harvard University Press.

De Souza P. 1999. *Piracy in the Graeco-Roman World*. Cambridge, Cambridge University Press.

De Souza P. 2012. *The Greek and Persian Wars 499–386 BC*. London/New York, Routledge.

Dickinson O. 2006. *The Aegean from Bronze Age to Iron Age: Continuity and Change between the Twelfth and Eighth Centuries B.C.* London/New York, Routledge.

Drake B. L. 2012. 'The Influence of Climatic Change on the Late Bronze Age Collapse and the Greek Dark Ages', *Journal of Archaeological Science* 39.6: 1862–70.

Dueck D. 2012. *Geography in Classical Antiquity*. Cambridge, Cambridge University Press.

Freeman C. 1996. *Egypt, Greece and Rome: Civilizations of the Ancient Mediterranean*. Oxford, Oxford University Press.

Geus K. 2003. 'Space and Geography', in A. Erskine (ed.), *A Companion to the Hellenistic Culture*. Malden/Oxford/Melbourne/Berlin, Blackwell Publishing: 232–45.

Geus K. 2018. 'Greek and Greco-Roman Geography', in A. Jones and L. Taub (eds.), *The Cambridge History of Science. Vol. 1: Ancient Science*. Cambridge, Cambridge University Press: 402–12.

Green P. 1996. *The Greco-Persian Wars*. Berkeley/Los Angeles/London, University of California Press. (reprint).

Gruen E. S. 2011. *Rethinking the Other in Antiquity*. Princeton/Oxford, Princeton University Press.

Hall J. M. 2014. *A History of the Archaic Greek World, ca. 1200–479 BCE*. Chichester, Wiley Blackwell.

Hansen M. H. 1994. 'Polis, Civitas, Stadtstaat and City-State', in D. Whitehead (ed.), *From Political Architecture to Stephanus Byzantius: Sources for the Ancient Greek Polis*. Papers from the Copenhagen Polis Centre 1, Stuttgart, Steiner: 19–22.

Hansen M. H. 1997. 'The Polis as an Urban Centre: The Literary and Epigraphical Evidence', in H. H. Hansen (ed.), *The Polis as an Urban Centre and as a Political Community: Symposium August, 29–31, 1996*. Acts of the Copenhagen Polis Centre vol. 4. Copenhagen, Det Kongelige Danske Videnskabernes Selskab: 9–86.

Hansen M. H. 1998. *Polis and City-State: An Ancient Concept and its Modern Equivalent. Symposium*, January 9. Acts of the Copenhagen Polis Centre vol. 5, Copenhagen, Munksgaard.

Hansen M. H. 2000a. 'The Hellenic Polis', in H. H. Hansen (ed.), *A Comparative Study of Thirty City-State Cultures: An Investigation Conducted by the CPC*. Copenhagen, Reitzels Vorlag: 141–87.

Hansen M. H. (ed.) 2000b. *A Comparative Study of Thirty City-State Cultures: An Investigation Conducted by the CPC*. Copenhagen, Reitzels Vorlag.

Hansen M. H. 2000c. 'The Concepts of City-State and City-State Culture', In H. H. Hansen (ed.), *A Comparative Study of Thirty City-State Cultures: An Investigation Conducted by the CPC*. Copenhagen, Reitzels Vorlag: 11–34.

Hansen M. H. and Nielsen T. H. (eds.) 2004. *An Inventory of Archaic and Classical Poleis*. Oxford, Oxford University Press.

Harley J. B., Woodward D. and Aujac J. 1987a. 'The Foundations of Theoretical Cartography in Archaic and Classical Greece', in J. B. Harley and D. Woodward (eds.), *History of Cartography*, vol. 1. Chicago, University of Chicago Press, chapter 8: 130–47.

Harley J. B., Woodward D. and Aujac J. 1987b. 'The Growth of an Empirical Cartography in Hellenistic Greece', in J. B. Harley and D. Woodward (eds.), *History of Cartography*, vol. 1. Chicago, University of Chicago Press, chapter 9: 148–60.

Hartog F. 1988. *The Mirror of Herodotus: The Representation of the Other in the Writing of History*. Berkeley/Los Angeles/London, University of California Press.

Heckel W. and Tritle L. A. (eds.) 2009. *Alexander the Great: A New History*. Oxford, Wiley-Blackwell.

Horden P. and Purcell N. 2000. *The Corrupting Sea: A Study of the Mediterranean History*. Malden/Oxford/Carlton, Blackwell Publishing.

Hutton W. 2005. *Describing Greece: Landscape and Literature in the Periegesis of Pausanias*. Cambridge, Cambridge University Press.

Jacob C. 1991. *Géographie et ethnographie en Grèce ancienne*. Paris, Colin.

Landels J. G. 2000. *Engineering in the Ancient World* (new revised edition). London, Constable.

Lazenby J. F. 1993. *The Defence of Greece 490–470 B.C.* Oxford, Aris and Phillips.

MacInerney J. 2001. 'Ethnos and Ethnicity in Early Greece', in I. Malkin (ed.), *Ancient Perceptions of Greek Ethnicity*. Cambridge, Harvard University Press: 51–73.
Mac Sweeney N. (ed.) 2015. *Foundation Myths in Ancient Societies: Dialogues and Discourses*. Philadelphia, University of Pennsylvania Press.
Malkin I. 1987. *Religion and Colonization in Ancient Greece*. Leiden/New York/København/Köln, Brill.
Malkin I. 2011. *A Small Greek World*. Oxford, Oxford University Press.
Morgan C. 2003. *Early Greek States beyond the Polis*. London/New York, Routledge.
Morkot R. 1996. *The Penguin Historical Atlas of Ancient Greece*. London, Penguin.
Morrison J. S., Coates J. F. and Rankov N. B. 2000. *The Athenian Trireme: The History and Reconstruction of an Ancient Greek Warship* (2nd edition). Cambridge, Cambridge University Press.
Morton J. 2001. *The Role of the Physical Environment in Ancient Greek Seafaring*. Leiden, Brill.
Mynott J. 2013. *Thucydides: The War of the Peloponnesians and the Athenians*. Cambridge, Cambridge University Press.
Ober J. 1996. *The Athenian Revolution: Essays on Ancient Greek Democracy and Political Theory*. Princeton, Princeton University Press.
Osborne R. 1987. *Classical Landscape with Figures: The Ancient Greek City and its Countryside*. London, George Philip.
Rivers R. 2016. 'Can Archaeological Models Always Fulfil Our Prejudices?', in T. Brughmans, A. Collar and F. Coward (eds.), *The Connected Past*. Oxford, Oxford University Press: 123–47.
Romm J. S. 1992. *The Edges of the Earth in Ancient Thought*. Princeton, Princeton University Press.
Rutherford I. 2009. 'Network Theory and Theoric Networks', in I. Malkin, C. Costantakopoulou and K. Panagopoulou (eds.), *Greek and Roman Networks in the Mediterranean*. London/New York, Routledge: 24–38.
Severin T. 1987. *The Ulysses Voyage: Sea Search for the Odyssey*. New York, Dutton.
Shipley G. 2011. *Pseudo-Skylax's Periplous: The Circumnavigation of the Inhabited World*. Exeter, Bristol Phoenix Press.
Smith D. G. 2004. "Thucydides' Ignorant Athenians and the Drama of the Sicilian Expedition', *Syllecta Classica* 15: 33–70.
Snodgrass A. 1980. *Archaic Greece: The Age of Experiment*. Berkeley/Los Angeles, University of California Press.
Sommer M. 2009. 'Networks of Commerce and Knowledge in the Iron Age: The Case of the Phoenicians', in I. Malkin, C. Costantakopoulou and K. Panagopoulou (eds.), *Greek and Roman Networks in the Mediterranean*. London/New York, Routledge: 94–108.
Thiering M. 2012. 'Spatial Mental Models in Common Sense Geography', in K. Geus and M. Thiering (eds.), *Common Sense Geography and Mental Modelling*. Berlin, Max Planck Institute for the History of Science, MPIWG Preprint 426: 11–44.

Thomas R. 2000. *Herodotos in Context: Ethnography, Science and the Art of Persuasion*. Cambridge, Cambridge University Press.
Van der Heyden A. A. M. and Scullard H. H. 1963. *Atlas of the Classical World*. London, Nelson.
Vegetti M. 1989. *L'etica degli antichi*. Bari, Laterza.
Vlassopoulos K. 2009. 'Beyond and Below the Polis: Networks, Associations, and the Writing of Greek History', in I. Malkin, C. Costantakopoulou and K. Panagopoulou (eds.), *Greek and Roman Networks in the Mediterranean*. London/New York, Routledge: 12–23.
Whitley J. 2001. *The Archaeology of Ancient Greece*. Cambridge World Archaeology. Cambridge, Cambridge University Press.
Wilson J.-P. 2006. '"Ideologies" of Greek Colonization', in G. Bradley and J.-P. Wilson (eds.), *Greek and Roman Colonization: Origins, Ideologies and Interactions*. Swansea, The Classical Press of Wales: 25–57.

4 Ancient Rome

Caesar (...) had resolved to cross the Rhine; but to cross by ships he neither deemed to be sufficiently safe, nor considered consistent with his own dignity or that of the Roman people. Therefore, although the greatest difficulty in forming a bridge was presented to him, on account of the breadth, rapidity, and depth of the river, he nevertheless considered that it ought to be attempted by him, or that his army ought not otherwise to be led over. (...) Within ten days after the timber began to be collected, the whole work was completed, and the whole army led over. (...) Having spent altogether eighteen days beyond the Rhine, and thinking he had advanced far enough to serve both honour and interest, he returned into Gaul, and cut down the bridge.

(Caes., *BGall.* 4.17–19)

Expansion

Environments

If we adopt here the same method that we have used for Egypt and Greece, and look at the territory that was once part of the Roman Empire from Google Earth, it is immediately clear that we are facing a more complex situation: in this case, we are looking at an incredibly vast territory, including plains, mountains, woods, marshes, deserts, rivers, and the entire Mediterranean, including the sea itself, not only the coasts (Figure 4.1).

At its fullest extent, the Roman Empire, centred on modern Italy, included modern Spain, Portugal, France, Belgium, a portion of the Netherlands, one of Germany, Switzerland, most of Austria, part of Hungary, part of Romania, Slovenia, Croatia, Bosnia-Herzegovina, Montenegro, Kosovo, Serbia, Bulgaria, Macedonia, Albania, Greece, Turkey, Lebanon, Syria, Jordan, most of Iraq, a portion of Saudi Arabia, Lebanon, Israel, Palestine, Egypt, and the coasts of Libya, Tunisia, Algeria, and Morocco.

88 *Ancient Rome*

Figure 4.1 Physical map of the territory under Roman rule, from Google Earth.

Ancient Rome 89

This vast territory was divided into provinces of various sizes: some corresponded to self-contained geographical zones, while others were named after their geographical position and often corresponding to different phases of conquest (Gallia Cisalpina, Transalpina/Narbonensis, Lugdunensis, and Belgica). Some provinces (e.g. Hispania, Illyricum, and Pannonia) were subdivided or redesigned for administrative purposes. In the late III century CE Diocletian reorganised both the administration and the army of the entire empire: he first grouped the existing provinces into new administrative units called dioceses, and then subdivided them into nearly one hundred new provinces (Southern 2001: 163–7).

Probably those who, more than anyone else, experienced the extremely different environments that the Roman Empire embraced were the soldiers, who travelled on foot, laden with weapons and supplies, across marshes, woods, rivers, and deserts. When reading between the lines of Caesar's account of his campaigns in Gaul and Britain, the dangers and the harshness of the life of ordinary soldiers emerge from the background. At sea, for instance:

> it happened that night to be full moon, which usually occasions very high tides in that ocean; and that circumstance was unknown to our men. (…) A great many ships having been wrecked (…), a great confusion, as would necessarily happen, arose throughout the army; for there were no other ships in which they could be conveyed back, and (…) corn for the winter had not been provided in those places, because it was understood by all that they would certainly winter in Gaul.
> (Caes., *BGall.* 4.29)

Or in the middle of Europe:

> Caesar marches into the country of the Helvii, although mount Cevennes, which separates the Arverni from the Helvii, blocked up the way with very deep snow, as it was the severest season of the year; yet having cleared away the snow to the depth of six feet, and having opened the roads, he reaches the territories of the Arverni, with infinite labor to his soldiers. This people being surprised, because they considered themselves defended by the Cevennes as by a wall, and the paths at this season of the year had never before been passable even to individuals, he orders the cavalry to extend themselves as far as they could, and strike as great a panic as possible into the enemy.
> (Caes., *BGall.* 7.8)

If we compare these words with the mute aerial photographs of the chain of Roman forts built along the roads that crossed harsh, dry, and remote desert

90 Ancient Rome

areas of the Middle East (Kennedy and Riley 1990), we gain a complete picture of the extreme environmental conditions that could be encountered across the vast expanse of the empire – a situation significantly different from that of Egypt and Greece, described in the previous chapters.

Ways of incorporation

Pinpointing a precise reason explaining the vertiginous rise of Rome is difficult. Born in the middle of the VIII century BCE as a village along the River Tiber, a river flowing across central Italy into the Tyrrhenian Sea, by the V century BCE it had grown into a small city, one of the many that punctuated the Italian peninsula. At that time, Italy was occupied by a mosaic of populations, some stationed along the coasts and some inland, each controlling a relatively small territory: from the Etruscans that ruled over a hilly portion of central Italy, to the Osco-Umbrian groups that extended their interests over the central mountainous region, and from the Celtic populations that overflew into the northern plain from the Alps, to the Greek colonies located all along the southern coasts (Mackay 2004: chapter 1; Scarre 1995: 12–25; see also Van der Heyden and Scullard 1963: 93).

Rome progressively gained an important position in the league of Latin populations, and eventually became their leader (Mackay 2004: chapter 2); it then started to 'absorb' other populations thanks to the Roman citizenship, 'a legal relation capable of expansion in great variations of form and status' (Van der Heyden and Scullard 1963: 96). This and the creation of the army, probably the most efficient in the entire ancient world, were the powerful tools thanks to which Rome set to conquer the world (cf. Bintliff 2010: 37–9).

In about eighty years (340–264 BCE) Rome managed to extend its rule over most of the Italian peninsula and started not only to challenge the populations stationed in the northern plain at the foot of the Alps, but also to represent a threat to the Carthaginian rule over the Eastern Mediterranean (Scarre 1995: 20–5). In the space of one further century, the Mediterranean was conquered (Mackay 2004: part two): Carthage was defeated and destroyed, and its territories annexed, including Hispania and a portion of the African coast (Figure 4.2). Then Rome acquired Greece, Macedonia, Cilicia, and Syria; Egypt became a Roman province at the death of Cleopatra VII, in the year 30 BCE. Northern Gallia was subdued in the I century BCE, all the way to the river Rhine (cf. Van der Heyden and Scullard 1963: 104); slightly later the Danube was reached and became the empire's north-eastern frontier. By the beginning of the II century CE the Roman Empire reached its maximum territorial extent, covering over five million km^2 (Figure 4.3), and that was more or less maintained for one full century (Goldsworthy 2000: 149–50).

The rapid success of Rome in the Mediterranean was already the subject of discussions in Antiquity. The Greek historian Polybius, who wrote his *Historiai* in the I century BCE, attributed its success to its constitution, which created a great unity in Roman society (Polyb. 6.18). Whether this was a philosophical or a historical consideration (cf. Davidson 1991; Walbank 1943; see also Mattingly 2011: chapter 1), it does reflect the ability of Rome to combine different elements into a single, working system. This is true also in geographical terms: during its unstoppable growth, the Roman power swallowed everything: lands, seas, rivers, plains, villages, and cities. It imposed on the Mediterranean world a significant change of scale, never seen before. The Persian Empire and the short-lived 'Macedonian Empire' pieced together by Alexander the Great involved only a small part of the Mediterranean area. Rome, located right in the middle of it, expanded from there in a solid and stable way, by progressively absorbing and extending habits and infrastructures in the newly conquered territories, thus truly incorporating them into an effective network.

Perhaps a clue to its success can be traced back to its original position: located on a small plain surrounded by seven hills, Rome started its existence by controlling a bridge on the river located just downstream from a small island, that marked the last point that could be reached by vessels coming upstream from the sea; there, a north–south route met another route heading east (Van der Heyden and Scullard 1963: 92). Titus Livius, in the I century BCE, wrote that:

> not without good reason did gods and men choose this spot as the site of a city, with its bracing hills, its commodious river, by means of which the produce of inland countries may be brought down and oversea supplies obtained; a sea near enough for all useful purposes, but not so near as to be exposed to danger from foreign fleets; a district in the very centre of Italy – in a word, a position singularly adapted by nature for the expansion of a city (*ad incrementum urbis natum unice locum*).
> (Liv. *Ab urbe cond.* 5.54)

Of course, settling in a 'convenient' spot, characterised by both agricultural potential and efficient connections, was what all settlers tried to do, and had been by no means an exclusive of tiny Rome in its beginnings. It is interesting, however, that Titus Livius, looking back, *ex post* picked up the variety of possible interconnections as the trigger for the city's expansion. Born on a crossroad of land- and waterways, Rome managed to turn the rather commonplace strategy of building and exploiting connections into a successful instrument to expand its power.

92　*Ancient Rome*

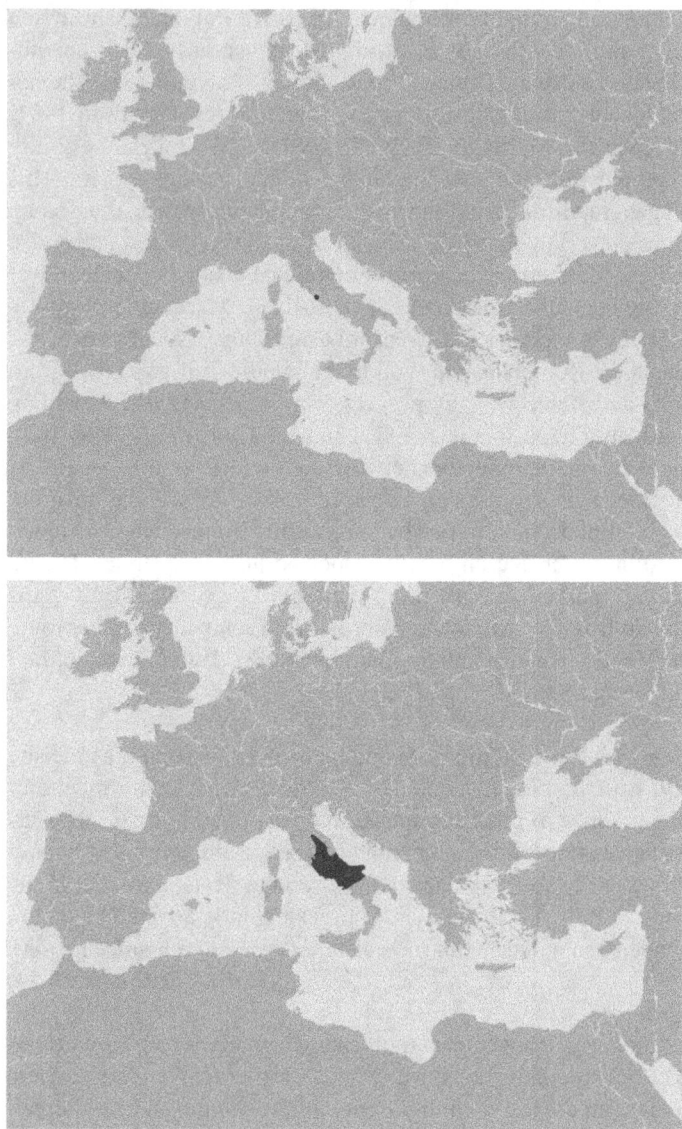

Figure 4.2a Progressive expansion of the Roman territory: 700 and 500 BCE.

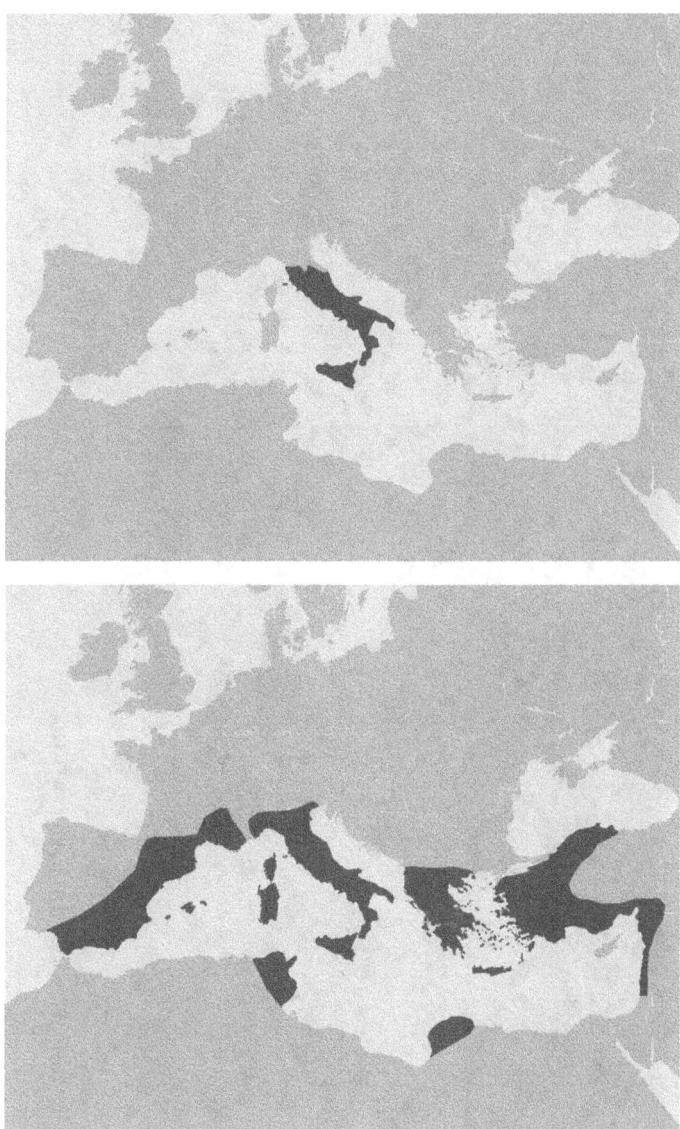

Figure 4.2b (Continued) The Roman territory in 240 and 60 BCE.

94 *Ancient Rome*

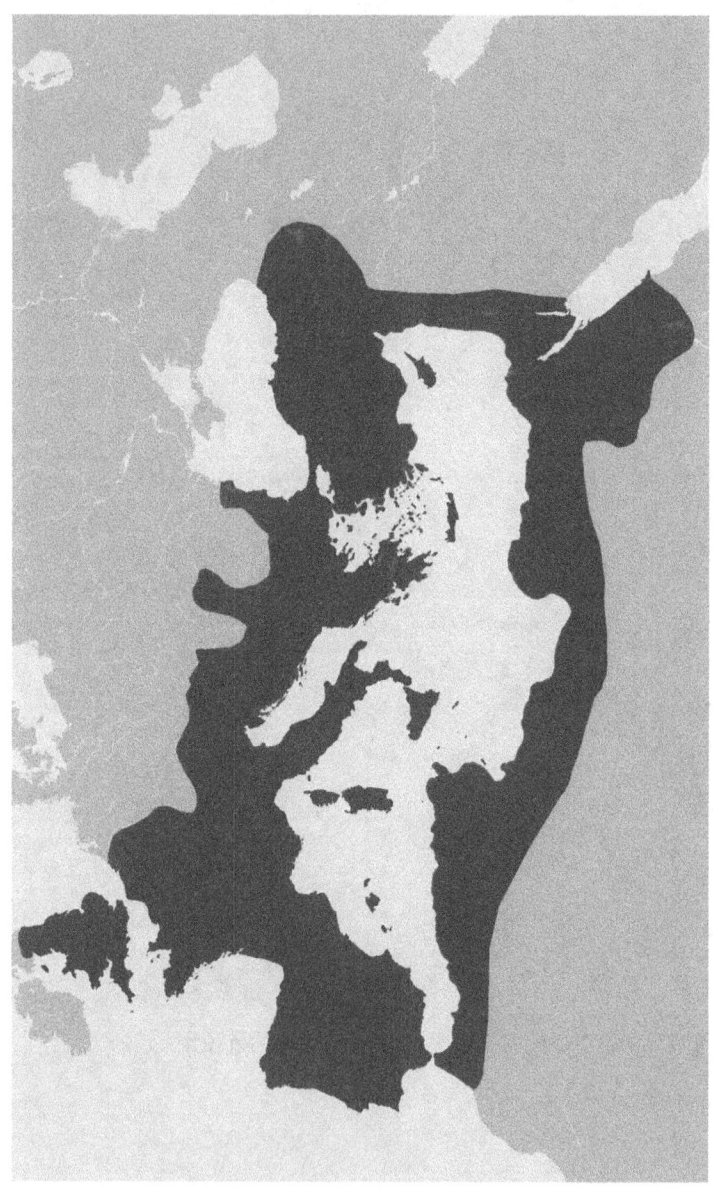

Figure 4.3 Maximum extent of the Roman Empire in AD 117.

Rome's system of power, based on efficiently moving people, objects, and information, maintained its efficacy and efficiency also when the scale of the operations grew exponentially (cf. Bintliff 2010: 37). Creating an efficient network of connections of various types (ranging from attributing roles and titles to building physical links deeply rooted into the local territory but well connected with other areas of the empire) represented the key to expanding a superior power over any particular situation, by incorporating the latter into the former and creating a general sense of belonging (cf. Hitchner 2012).

That a new world was being shaped by the Roman expansion was clear: in the II century BCE, Polybius explicitly declared that 'his work was directed towards exploring the way in which Roman power had spread to the extent that world history would cease to be spatially subdivided' (Clarke 1999: 341–3). One century later, when the rise of Augustus marked the official birth of the Roman Empire, in his *Geographika* (that mixes elements that we would today classify separately as historical and geographical) Strabo described a world that had been unified by the unstoppable rise of Rome. The universalism that transpires from his literary work perfectly matches and expresses the imperialism of Rome (Nicolet 1991: chapters 5 and 8; Clarke 1999: chapter 6).

Frontiers

The Roman state grew exponentially in geographical terms until the birth of the empire, after which the pace of its expansion slowed down; it reached and managed to keep its maximum extent between the II and the early III centuries CE, with the alternating addition and loss of some peripheral areas.

The frontiers of the territory under Roman rule have been the subject of long debate. The modern habit to mark frontiers by lines on maps conveys the impression of a clear demarcation between two entities, but during the expansion phase this was only partly true: in that period the frontiers were mainly transition zones between the area under direct and firm Roman rule to areas under the influence of other populations, where a whole range of activities could take place, including explorations of unknown territories, military raids, diplomatic trips, and spying activities, as well as operations of import and export (Nicolet 1991: chapter 4; Goldsworthy 2000: 146; Elton 1996: 3–5, chapter IV, and 111–3; also Luttwak 1999: 8; Lee 1993; Austin and Rankov 1995; see Whittaker 2004: 5–6 for a discussion on the terms 'frontiers' and 'boundaries').

Looking on a map, it can be easily noted that the expansion phase basically stopped when the borders of the Roman Empire reached major natural features marking a discontinuity: the Atlantic Ocean to the west, the Sahara to the south, and the major rivers the Rhine and Danube to the north-east. The presence of natural lines of demarcation certainly played an important role, and still do: the Rhine still marks part of the boundary between modern France and Germany, while sections of the Danube mark the modern borders between Serbia and Romania, Serbia and Croatia, Slovakia and Hungary, as well as Germany and Austria. However, natural obstacles are just part of a wider and more complex picture in which connectivity and political choices played an equally important role.

The Rhine gained its role as a frontier under Caesar, the first to reach that area in a military campaign: the difficulty of crossing such a large river, both on the Roman and on the Germanic side, transpires quite clearly from the *De Bello Gallico*, in which Caesar himself describes his enterprise (Caes., *BGall.* 4.16–19). The short-lived attempt, dating to the I century CE, to move the frontier from the River Rhine to the River Elbe, located 300 km to the east, was abandoned after the scorching defeat suffered by the legions led by Varus. In the following years, the Romans often crossed the Rhine and inflicted heavy damages and losses to the local population in revenge, but never attempted again to permanently expand beyond the river (Goldsworthy 2000: 111).

Rivers were accepted as borders between Roman provinces or between Roman and foreign territories, but 'there seems to have been no official nature to these characterisations' (Elton 1996: 4). Mountains, too, acted as markers to establish boundaries, even if to a lesser extent. At any rate, both rivers and mountains shared one important characteristic: they were all physical obstacles to travellers, and therefore to the transport of goods, people, and information (cf. Lee 1993: 49–50). In fact, the importance of bridges was paramount: the architectural masterpiece built in the early II century CE by the emperor Trajan over the Danube to carry out a massive military invasion of Dacia was taken down a few decades later by Hadrian, fearing that it could be used the other way around, by the Dacians to invade Roman territories. Eventually, keeping Dacia within the empire proved to be too difficult, as that territory had to be defended on three sides, and around 270 CE the Romans retreated again to the south of the Danube (Parker 2010: 259 and 272).

Not all rivers, however, worked well as boundaries: to the east, for instance, the Euphrates was meant to act as a border between the Roman and the Parthian superpowers, but never really functioned as such (Elton 1996: 4). The long stand-off was due to a combination of reasons, among which the fact that the two armies followed two completely different combat methods: the Parthian cavalry often adopted the solution of fleeing if the situation became unfavourable, only to then unexpectedly turn back and hit the pursuers, mainly consisting of infantry. In this situation, after a first battle at Carrhae won by the Parthians, the Romans did not manage to force the enemy to face them in a single, major battle, and the Parthians did not manage to stop the Roman army from advancing into their territory. Eventually, the need to pour into the final conquest a large amount of wealth and the necessity to engage a commander away from Rome for years discouraged the Romans, who abandoned the effort (Goldsworthy 2000: 132–5).

Only in some cases, in the absence of natural physical boundaries, did the Romans revert to the construction of artificial barriers, such as Hadrian's Wall and the Antonine Wall in Britain, the Antonine Frontier in Germania Superior, and the *Fossatum Africae* in Numidia (Luttwak 1999: 60 and map 2.1). Most of the empire's frontier, however, did not rely on artificial demarcations.

The Roman rule expanded until it could keep a balance between physical, military, and political factors. The Sahara was not really impenetrable to human occupation, but the first major elements of potential Roman interest (be they commercial partners or potential enemies of a certain consistency) lay at a discouraging distance of weeks of dangerous and fatiguing journeys, and the small-scale raids periodically launched by the nomadic populations stationed along the desert fringe, although annoying, could be evidently contained within tolerable limits (Elton 1996: 101–3). Expanding the Roman infrastructures into such a harsh environment was just not worth the effort. This might be the same conclusion that the Romans reached in Britain, when they decided to abandon the idea to conquer the northernmost region (Parker 2010: 5–6). Seemingly, subduing the German tribes or defeating Parthia was technically feasible, but would have required the emperor to attribute a substantial power to military commanders who could later turn into political rivals (Goldsworthy 2000: 115).

Political and military reasons rested on the same foundation: the physical shape of the territory. The fact that most of the borders of the Roman Empire corresponded to natural boundaries is the obvious consequence of the fact that territories, in order to be managed and exploited, need to be reached and crossed in a relatively easy way. Physical boundaries might not be the sole reason why the empire stopped there, but they certainly helped to shape and maintain it.

Travelling by land

Roads

Connections on land depended on the existence of usable roads, and the Romans proudly invested in this direction from the earliest phases of their expansion. The first roads to be built were the *Via Salaria* and the *Via*

Tiberina, which ran along the valley of the Tiber and marked the stages of the occupation of the region Latium (Adam 2001: 276). The scale and aim of road building stepped up with the construction of the *Via Appia*, the *regina viarum* ('queen of the roads'), heading first to Capua and later to Brindisi, from where it was possible to sail eastwards across the Adriatic Sea. It was followed by the *Via Flaminia*, which took its name from Caius Flaminius and reached Fano on the Adriatic coast, following an ingenious path across the Apennine mountains, which avoided passes that were clogged by snow during the winter season. Both roads took their names from the commissioners of public works who were in charge when their construction was started, respectively Appius Claudius in 312 BCE, and Caius Flaminius in 220 BCE. A few years later, the *Via Aemilia*, named after the consul Marcus Aemilius Lepidus, continued the *Via Flaminia* to Piacenza and then Milan; the II century also saw the construction of another major road, the *Via Aurelia*, which ran along the Tyrrhenian coast all the way to Genova.

From this initial core, a web of major and minor roads was extended over the newly conquered territories, in the north, east, west, and south, across the Mediterranean (Casson 1994: chapter 10). By the I century CE, the Roman road network was made of *viae publicae* ('public roads'), built by the state and bearing the name of the officer who ordered their construction; *viae militares* ('military roads') built by and for the army, that later became public roads (see, for instance, the evolution of the *Via Egnatia* in Lolos 2009); and *viae privatae* ('private roads', Adam 2001: 276–7). At its peak, the Roman road network included an estimated 80,000 km of paved and well-maintained roads, with the addition of 320,000 km of secondary routes (Figure 4.4; Sidebotham, Hense, and Nouwens 2008: 46). A large-scale infrastructure, it survived the empire and shaped the development of various regions well after the fall of the Roman Empire (Dalgaard et al. 2018).

Roman roads were generally well built: archaeological investigations revealed that stone foundations were generally covered by a layer of sand and gravel, and finished by compact layers of pebbles or flat stones, laid out following a curving profile that caused rainwater to discharge into ditches running along their edges. Paved roads were indicated as *viae silice stratae*, from which derive the modern words *strada* (Italian), *street* (English), *straat* (Dutch), and *straße* (German). Stable, solid, and drained, these roads could be used throughout the entire year (Casson 1994: 166). In the case of roads running across marshy areas, the paved section rested on a wooden platform fixed into the ground at regular intervals (Adam 2001: 277); roads running across the desert, instead, were rarely paved and consisted mainly of strips of terrain that had been thoroughly cleared of pebbles and stones, which were accumulated along its edges and visually marked the way

Ancient Rome 99

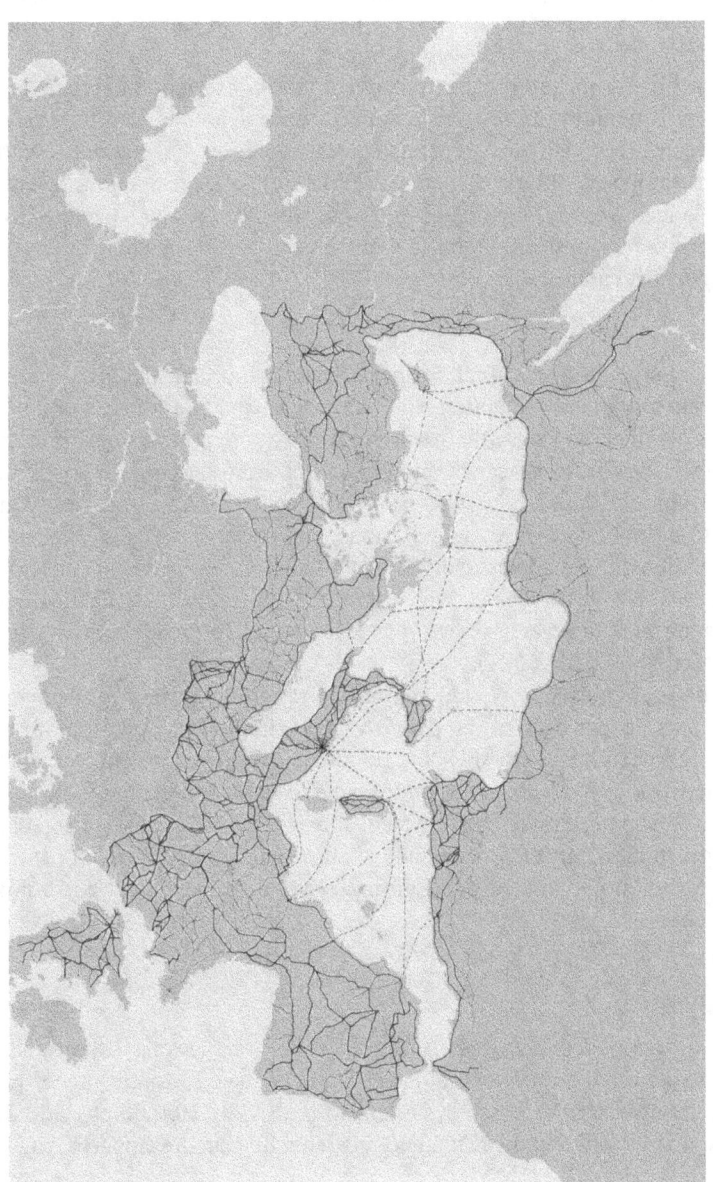

Figure 4.4 Simplified map of the main roads crossing the Roman Empire. The thicker line represents the *Itinerarium Antonini*.

(Sidebotham, Hense, and Nouwens 2008: 44). In some cases, the physical remains of the roads are less well preserved and more difficult to retrieve, and yet can be still reconstructed by piecing together information from various sources (e.g. Güimil-Fariña and Parcero-Oubiña 2015).

Roads generally pointed straight to their destination: in the I century CE Plutarchos, recounting the life of the tribune Caius Gracchus, wrote that:

> he busied himself most earnestly with the construction of roads, laying stress upon utility, as well as upon that which conduced to grace and beauty. For his roads were carried straight through the country without deviation (…). Depressions were filled up, all intersecting torrents or ravines were bridged over, and both sides of the roads were of equal and corresponding height, so that the work had everywhere an even and beautiful appearance.
>
> (Plut., *C. Gracc.* 7.1)

Heading straight to the final destination was important, but great care was also taken to avoid the bottom of valleys that could be flooded or covered by snow: in some cases, the roads ran halfway up on the sides, preferring a longer but always accessible itinerary over a shorter but potentially more problematic path (Casson 1994: 166–7). Roads running across desert areas had to be provided with water stations, and in some cases with protected rest-stations; the roads crossing Egypt's Eastern Desert, for instance, were endowed with *hydreumata* (water stations) and *praesidia* (fortified enclosures surrounding water stations) at regular intervals (Sidebotham, Hense, and Nouwens 2008: 50–1).

Roads are correctly considered one of the most distinctive elements of the Roman expansion: ruling over a vast world was only possible if reaching any part of it was feasible, and relatively easy. The existence of a physical network of roads does not imply the existence of an equally ubiquitous and widespread network of physical movements of people and goods in any given moment (cf. Brughmans, Collar, and Coward 2016: 8). It rather represented a network of possibilities, ready to be exploited according to the need.

Itineraria

Moving people, goods, and information across the vast expanse of an empire required a strict organisation. The Persians, for instance, relied on a very efficient dispatch system, also praised by Herodotos (Hdt. 8.98; Casson 1994: 54–5 and 182). Suetonius recounts that the emperor Augustus established a first system of transmission of information, known as *cursus publicus* (Kolb 2001):

> In order to obtain the earliest intelligence of what was passing in the provinces, he established posts, consisting at first of young men stationed at moderate distances along the military roads, and afterwards of regular couriers with fast vehicles; which appeared to him the most commodious, because the persons who were the bearers of dispatches, written on the spot, might then be questioned about the business, as occasion occurred.
> (Suet., *Aug.* 49)

The strict organisation of official movements across the empire remained a constant over the centuries. In the IV century CE, Ambrose wrote that:

> The soldier who is setting out on a journey does not organise his own travel arrangements, nor does he choose his route by his own judgement, nor chase after the pleasurable shortcuts, lest he slip away from the standards; rather he takes his itinerary from his commander and keeps to that: he proceeds according to the prescribed stages, travelling with his weapons, and makes the journey by the right route, so that he will find the assistance for his journeyings already prepared. (…) An army travels for three days, on the fourth day it rests.
> (Ambrose *Expositio psalmi* CXVIII 5.2, Salway 2001: 37)

Travelling by land was more tiring and time-consuming than travelling by sea, even if less dependent on the weather conditions. Travellers on land were encumbered by their heavy luggage, consisting of clothes, supplies, and personal goods; the major Roman roads were good enough to allow the use of pack animals and wagons, for those who could afford them. Inns and hostels of the *cursus publicus* were not specifically meant only for travellers engaged in official business, and could also host independent travellers, in case of availability of space. As travellers meant business, independent rest-stations flourished anywhere along the roads, often triggering the birth of a settlement around them, and bore meaningful names such as *Rufini Taberna* ('Rufinus' Inn'), *Ad Stabulum* ('By the Country Inn'), and *Tres Tabernae* (Three Inns) on the Appian Way. Central Europe is punctuated by place names that betray similar origins: *tabernae* ('the inns') is the common root of the modern names of Zabern, Saverne, Tavers, Tavernières, and Tavernolles, to name just a few (Casson 1994: chapters 11 and 12, esp. 201).

102 *Ancient Rome*

The information collected for administrative and military purposes was probably on display as a public lists of distances, called *tabellaria*, from which it was possible to draw *itineraria* (itineraries), that is, lists of places and distances to be covered to reach a specific destination. There is ample evidence of the use of such documents in the Roman period: some surviving documents describe private journeys, such as the so-called *Itinerarium Burdigalense* (describing a pilgrimage from Gaul to Jerusalem), whereas the *Itinerarium Antonini* aimed at offering a global glance of the travel network of the entire empire (cf. figure 4.4). The latter is a written list of destinations and intervening distances; the place names do not appear in nominative, but in oblique cases, reflecting the structure of sentence running according to the scheme '(from a) certain place, (to) another, (to) another, and so on to the final destination' (Salway 2001: 30).

The first entry of the *Itinerarium Antonini* concerning the province of Italia describes the journey from *Mediolanum* (Milan) to 'Columna', the column that was once placed near modern Reggio Calabria and that marked the closest point of the coast from Sicily, where it was therefore more convenient to board a ship to cross the strait (cf. Str. 6.1.5). The distances are given in Roman miles here abbreviated as *mpm*. It starts thus:

Iter quod a Mediolano per Picenum et Campaniam ad Columnam, id est Traiectum Siciliae ducit	*mpm DCCCCLVI (sic)*
A Mediolano Laude civitas	*mpm XVI*
Placentia civitas	*mpm XXIIII*
Fidentiola vicus	*mpm XXIIII*
Parma civitas	*mpm XV*
Regio civitas	*mpm XVIII*
(…)	

After listing thirty-four other stations and landmarks, the journey reaches its final destination, after surpassing two last rivers:

Ad fluvium Sabatum	*mpm XVIII*
Ad Turris	*mpm XVIII*
Ad fluvium Angitulam	*mpm XIII*
Nicotera	*mpm XXV*
Ad Mallias	*mpm XXIIII*
Ad Columnam	*mpm XIIII*

Land itineraries appear to somehow mirror the Greek *periploi*. Both are written descriptions of journeys actually made by someone, schematised into the basic information necessary to replicate them: from here to there, followed by the distance. The latter was provided in the most logical way for the traveller: days at sea for the Greeks, miles for the Roman traveller,

Ancient Rome 103

but leagues too, in Gaul, for those travelling across that land (Salway 2001: 26).

All these documents were meant for people who set out on what was always a lengthy journey by modern standards, either sailing on a ship, or walking, or riding along a road, or combining all these methods; they were exposed to cold and hot weather, to the sun, rain, wind, ice, waves, and tides, but thanks to the experiences of previous travellers, recorded and somehow codified into these written documents, they proceeded trusting that the following rest-station lay not far away.

Representations

Our knowledge of maps drawn in the Roman period derives from a combination of sources, among which the maps themselves represent only a small part, as they are mainly lost.

To the II century CE dates the work of Claudios Ptolemaios, who lived, studied, and worked in Alexandria. His treatises *Mathematike Syntaxis* ('Mathematical Syntaxis', also known as *Almagest*) and *Geographike Hyphegesis* ('Geographical Instructions') appear to have had little impact at the time they were produced; for thirteen centuries they remained dormant, until they were rediscovered in the XV century and became a cornerstone of European cartography. As already mentioned above, it is unclear whether or not the original text was accompanied by maps, whether they were large or small, and if and how they incorporated regional maps that might have local origins (Dilke, Harley, and Woodward 1987: 177–8).

His work aimed at constructing a geometrical model of the Earth and placing the *oikoumene* into it. Drawn to a much smaller scale and for a more practical purpose, cadastral maps belonged to the same realm, that is, the geometric appropriation of the land (Dilke 1987a: 209–11; 1987b: 212–5; Cuomo 2001: 154–7), that obviously overlapped with, implemented, and implied a political appropriation (see also Nicolet 1991: chapters 6 and 7). The division of the land into plots was called *centuriatio*, which etymologically refers to the practice of dividing an area into one hundred (*centum*) parts. Land-surveying was a major factor in Roman expansion: North Africa, for instance, was extensively centuriated as well as provided with roads, bridges, aqueducts, and geometrically planned towns (Cuomo 2007: 103 ff.). Cadastral maps helped measure the land across which the *centuriatio* was laid out, although they might lead to cumulative errors in the total distances (Dilke, Harley, and Woodward 1987: 196).

All these maps consist of geometrical patterns superimposed on the land, and only indirectly represented the territory itself. The work of Claudios Ptolemaios, in fact, was never meant to directly support travellers

(Dilke 1987c: 254), but was rather meant to grasp dimensions and geometry of the Earth and sky. It might have inspired representations of the known world, as was perhaps the case with a world map, an *orbis pictus*, on display in a school in Augustodunum in Gaul in the III century (Talbert 2012: 170–2). Although geometrised maps became part of high-level education in the Roman world, other types of representations also survived, including flat discs (Harley, Woodward, and Aujac 1987: 167–72; see also Dan et al. 2016).

Since the earliest period, Roman maps were mainly 'concerned in various ways with geographical expansion or with the organisation and exploitation of settled lands thus brought under political control' (Dilke 1987a: 205). In the late Republican period, when the expansion of Roman rule became substantial, maps certainly also gained a role within administration and propaganda. During the empire, cartography became progressively more detached from geometry (Dilke 1987c: 234), and gained more importance as an instrument to communicate not only the growing knowledge of the known world (Dilke, Harley, and Woodward 1987), but also the power and extent of the Roman rule: the lost Map of Agrippa, exposed in the Porticus Vipsania, in Rome, probably consisted of a drawing of the entire *orbis terrarum* (thus not only the *orbis Romanus*) illustrating the information contained in an accompanying written text (Tierney 1962–1964; Nicolet 1991: chapter 5). This map followed a well-known tradition of associating pictorial illustration and public porticos, dating back to V century BCE Athens, and was probably meant to present the known world for political and educational purposes, an operation of propaganda promoted by the emperor Augustus himself (Dilke 1987a: 207; Nicolet 1991: 5–9 and chapter 8).

The most famous map of the Roman Empire is the *Tabula Peutingeriana*: known from a medieval copy, it represented its entire territory and all the main roads that criss-crossed it. It contains both Pompeii, destroyed by the eruption of Vesuvius in 79 BCE, and Constantinopolis, founded in the IV century CE, thus suggesting that it combined information from significantly different dates (Dilke 1987c: 238–42; Brodersen 2001: 18), perhaps as a result of progressive additions to an original set of data. This map had not been conceived to offer precise instructions to travellers en route, and yet the jagged lines that run across the eleven sections of the map, representing itineraries heading from station to station, clearly indicate that the empire was defined by the existence and extent of these roads. As a comprehensive illustration of the connections existing across the Roman Empire, the map conveyed a powerful impression of the Roman organisation and control over its territory (Talbert 2010: 142–57).

The problem of the deformations in the representation of the lands, on which Claudios Ptolemaios focused his attention, was clearly not an issue in this case (Dilke, Harley, and Woodward 1987: 192–7). The main focus of the *Tabula Peutingeriana* appears to be the road network itself, and the section that includes Rome perfectly reflects the proverb *omnes viae Romam ducunt* ('all roads lead to Rome'). As in the *Itinerarium Antonini*, here also the place names appear in oblique cases, reflecting the movement of the traveller from one place to another (Salway 2001: 30). There must have been a continuous flow of information between local, specific itineraries (written and/or drawn) and larger or diverse collections of information (cf. Whittaker 2004: 76–8): geographical handbooks listing places and features were meant as reference works to better understand literary texts, while itineraries listing (sequences of) places were meant to help travellers; maps are likely to have been involved, but their role remains unclear (Lee 1993: 80–90).

Differently from celebrative maps, drawings specifically meant to support travellers are likely to have been focused on much smaller portions of terrain. An interesting passage by Vegetius (Veg. *Mil.* 3.6), dating to the late IV century CE, states that:

> (having *itineraria*) accurately described, he [a commander] might take into account shortcuts, branch-roads, hills and rivers. More ingenious commanders are claimed to have had itineraries of the areas in which their attention was required not so much annotated (*non tantum adnotata*) but even illustrated (*sed etiam picta*), so that the road for setting out on might be chosen not only by a mental consideration but truly at a glance of the eyes.
>
> (Salway 2001: 31)

Drawings would have clearly helped travellers to orient themselves and find their way, and their use is likely to be much older than the Roman period: the XXII century BCE itinerary to reach the mining settlement of Umm al-Fawakhir in Egypt's Eastern Desert, described in Chapter 2, may belong to the same type of documents.

These drawings, whether they illustrated specific areas or large territories, were meant to convey information on the places – collected, perceived, and used from a subjective point of view. It is interesting to note that the division of the Roman Empire into a *Pars Occidentalis* and a *Pars Orientalis*, instead, must have been traced on a map constructed on a spatial grid. The neat north–south 'vertical' cut is unlikely to be the result of someone looking at a 'propaganda' map like the *Tabula Peutingeriana*: it is more likely that a 'technical' map based on the efforts of Claudios Ptolemaios was involved in the matter. This would imply that (what we perceive as) different 'descriptions of the earth' were used at the same time, depending on the scope.

Keeping the empire

Roads and conquests

Roads were measured in Roman miles, corresponding to a value of c. 1,480 m. The modern name of this unit of measurement comes straight from the Latin *mille passuum*, that is, one thousand paces (counted every other pace, that is, every time the same foot struck the ground). Therefore, their length referred to someone walking, and counting as he went on. The modern word 'mile' (and its equivalents in other languages), even if referring to slightly different numerical values, retains however the memory of the original, physical interaction between people and territory.

Roads were necessary to reach any part of the territory under Roman rule; actually, we may also remix and integrate the sentence: roads were necessary, first of all, to reach territories *and place them* under Roman rule – and then to keep them there. In this earlier sense, roads represent the foundation and the backbone of the conquest of Gaul by Julius Caesar, a bold enterprise that lasted for eight years, from 58 to 51 BCE. The practical aspects of the military operations appear to have been his main focus: 'Caesar's own commentaries, in fact, were about how he conquered much of Western Europe, not why its conquest would be beneficial to Rome, or the costs and benefits – and future challenges – of its annexation' (Hanson 2010: 9).

Caesar's direct and indirect knowledge of the territory transpires from every sentence of his *De Bello Gallico*, and clearly represented a winning asset of the Roman army against the various tribes that populated the area. In particular, key was the knowledge of how to move across that territory, that is, the characteristics of the roads, and the position of bridges:

> there were in all two routes, by which they could go forth from their country: one through the Sequani, narrow and difficult, between Mount Jura and the river Rhone, by which scarcely one wagon at a time could be led; there was, moreover, a very high mountain overhanging, so that a very few might easily intercept them; the other, through our Province, much easier and freer from obstacles, because the Rhone flows between the boundaries of the Helvetii and those of the Allobroges, who had lately been subdued (...). The furthest town of the Allobroges, and the nearest to the territories of the Helvetii, is Geneva. From this town a bridge extends to the Helvetii. (...) When it was reported to Caesar that they were attempting to make their route through our Province he hastens to set out from the city, (...) and he orders the bridge at Geneva to be broken down.
>
> (Caes., *BGall.* 1.6–7)

Crossing rivers was always a difficult and crucial enterprise, as it exposed the armies to attack just when they were divided and unable to react in an efficient way:

> there is a river [called] the Saone, which flows through the territories of the Aedui and Sequani into the Rhone with such incredible slowness, that it cannot be determined by the eye in which direction it flows. This the Helvetii were crossing by rafts and boats joined together. When Caesar was informed by spies that the Helvetii had already conveyed three parts of their forces across that river, but that the fourth part was left behind on this side of the Saone, he set out from the camp with three legions during the third watch, and came up with that division which had not yet crossed the river. Attacking them encumbered with baggage, and not expecting him, he cut to pieces a great part of them; the rest betook themselves to flight, and concealed themselves in the nearest woods.
>
> (Caes., *BGall.* 1.12)

The army then had to be supplied: food, first of all, for both men and animals, as well as all other kinds of basic goods such as clothing and weapons. At the beginning of the V century CE, in his *De re militari*, Vegetius dedicated an entire paragraph to the crucial and critical task of providing forage and provisions:

> famine makes greater havoc in an army than the enemy, and is more terrible than the sword. (…) The main and principal point in war is to secure plenty of provisions and to destroy the enemy by famine. (…) An exact calculation must therefore be made before the commencement of the war as to the number of troops and the expenses incident thereto, so that the provinces may in plenty of time furnish the forage, corn, and all other kinds of provisions demanded of them to be transported.
>
> (Veg. *Mil.* 3.3.1)

Logistics lay at the basis of successful military campaigns (Kehne 2007: 334), and all this was made possible by the road network. It has been calculated that, in the second half of the II century CE, every year the army needed over 150,000 tons of wheat and over 100,000 tons of supplementary food for the men, and nearly 250,000 tons of barley and over 400,000 tons of hay for the animals (Kehne 2007: 325). All these provisions mainly came from the regions that were being occupied by the army, and were charged to the local population, who were also responsible for their transport to the final destination (cf. Whittaker 2004: 12). The need for additional goods and supplies quickly turned into new trading opportunities (Kehne 2007: 329); sometimes entire villages grew near military camps (Goldsworthy 2003: 105–7; see also Wells 1999: especially chapter 7). Not all roads were built for military or economic reasons (Carreras and De Soto 2013), but all of them were part of the same network that spread across the entire empire.

Roads and frontiers

The Latin word *limes* is generally used to identify the borders of the empire, especially the sections that were manned and fortified. Originally, however, the term apparently referred to a military road that allowed penetration into a foreign territory (Parker 2010: 3), thus describing a movement *across* the border, rather than the border itself. This obviously reflects the point that there is no occupation without presence, and therefore without the possibility of moving around: as Luttwak noted (1999: 60), 'the essential element of the *limes* was not the wall, palisade, or fence, but rather the network of roads linking the frontier garrison with one another and frontier zone as a whole with the interior'.

Major roads were certainly meant to allow large-scale movements across the empire. Under the Flavii, for instance, an extensive road network was constructed to connect the Danube region to the area of the Euphrates; it became a major thoroughfare for legions travelling in both directions during the II and III centuries, as was also witnessed by the presence of camel bones in Pannonia (Wheeler 2011: 246 and 258). Another example was the *Via Egnatia*, which stretched for nearly 800 km, from Apollonia, on the coast of modern Albania, to Constantinopolis; conceived as a military road to keep Macedonia under control, once the region was pacified it became part of the *cursus publicus* and acted as main communication channel, along which flourished business, trade, and social relations (Lolos 2009).

In the Near East, defensive roads specifically built to facilitate the rapid movements of troops include the II century CE *Via Nova Traiana*, which ran for 350 km in a north–south direction from Bosra, to the south of Damascus, to modern Aqaba on the Red Sea, and the IV century CE *Strata Diocletiana*, which ran at least from modern Damascus northwards to Sura on the Euphrates (Parker 2010: 314, 354, and 358). In Egypt, the *Via Hadriana*, built after 130 CE and punctuated by wells, stations, and garrisons, might have had different functions, including supporting trade between the Nile Valley and the Red Sea, transports from and to the quarries of the Eastern Desert, and military and administrative activities (Adams 2007: 42). In Egypt the network of roads worked alongside that of canals: the

Amnis Trajanus was meant to connect the city of Babylon (modern Cairo) to the newly founded city of Clysma on the Red Sea (Mayerson 1996). Two hundred years later, Diocletian built a fortress in Babylon spreading over the two sides of the canal, so as to stress the importance of controlling the waterway (Sheehan et al. 2018: 224–5).

As we have seen above, the territory under Roman rule grew rapidly at the beginning, then the pace slowed down in the early empire. During the first phase, some borders were rather blurred, due to the juxtaposition of areas under direct administrative control, with areas under political control and areas of mere influence (Luttwak 1999: 59–60). By the time of Hadrian, in the early II century, the limits of the empire became closer to resembling precise lines, which may be however described as being rather thick, as they often implied movements across areas of significant depth.

Apart from the major roads linking distant locations, the defence of the borders in this phase depended also on a network of minor roads, allowing the army to react and rapidly reach the areas where problems arose. The actual number of soldiers in charge of controlling the frontier areas was too small to intercept or prevent every raid. The army, however, could make sure that no attack would go unpunished: short raids were carried out in retaliation by lightly armed troops on the villages beyond the borders from where the raid originated, at the same time taking revenge on the perpetrators and discouraging them from trying again. In this way, the frontier zone was an area in which the army managed to keep a balance between the inevitable raids and their organised response (Goldsworthy 2000: 148–9; Luttwak 1999: 132–3).

Between the late III and the early IV century CE, a structural change in the organisation of the Roman army reached its maturity and became official: the army was divided into *limitanei* and *comitatenses*. The *limitanei* were soldiers settled along the *limes* (the *ripenses* being those settled along rivers), whereas the *comitatenses* were strong and fast-moving field armies, under direct imperial control, stationed in the rear of the frontier, ready to act in case they were summoned by the frontier troops (Whately 2015; Strobel 2001; Luttwak 1999; Southern and Dixon 1996: chapter 2). The defence was thus based not only on the presence of fortified settlements, fortification, and barriers along the frontier, but also on the presence of an efficient network of interconnecting roads.

Connectivity

Travelling across the territories under Roman rule implied combining land, river, and sea travels, in a continuum that spanned over the vast, central expanse of the Mediterranean Sea (Adams 2007: 7; Luttwak 1999: 81). The chessboard over which Caesar and Pompey fought the civil war between 49 and 45 BCE, for instance, corresponded to the entire Roman territory, and their actions were based on the possibility to gather information, collect armies, and organise transport to and from distant locations. In Caesar's own words:

> though Caesar was fully sensible that to finish the war at a blow he must pass the sea immediately and endeavour to come up with Pompey before he could draw his transmarine forces together, yet he dreaded the delay and length of time that such a project might require. Because Pompey having carried with him all the ships on the coast, rendered the present execution of the design impracticable. He must therefore wait the arrival of ships from Picenum, Sicily and the remoter coasts of Gaul, which was a tedious business, and, at that season of the year, subject to great uncertainty. (...) He determined, therefore, to lay aside, for the present, the design of pursuing Pompey.
> (Caes., *BCiv.* 1.29–30)

In a slight exaggeration, fully comprehensible from a political point of view, the territory across which the two competitors fought was described by various ancient authors as corresponding to the entire world (*orbis terrarum*, the Latin equivalent of the Greek *oikoumene*, Nicolet 1991: 29–34).

In general, sea transport could be faster than land transport, provided that the weather was favourable. The journey from Rome to Cologne would take sixty-seven days of marching time, while the navigation from Puteoli to Carthage took an average of ten days, but on lucky circumstances could be covered in two days only. The entire trip from Rome to Antioch on land took about 120 marching days, plus two days at sea to cross the Adriatic from Brundisium to Dyrrachium; the journey by sea from Puteoli to Antioch generally took about fifty-five days, but could be completed in fifteen (Luttwak 1999: 81–5 and map 2.2; see also the online resource Orbis, the Stanford Geospatial Network Model of the Roman World).

This was the (varying) speed at which everything travelled: people, goods, and information, although a simplified set of the latter could travel faster thanks to coded signals (fires lit on chains of towers, and the like, e.g. Southern 1990). Nowadays information travels in a nearly instantaneous way across most of the globe, but until telecommunications were invented, detailed information was physically transmitted by people, and therefore travelled with them. The transmission of information was, of course, a crucial element for maintaining Roman rule: background knowledge on the general situation was instrumental for administrative purposes, and strategic knowledge was essential for military control. All this was performed by a relatively small number of imperial administrators, in comparison with the enormous size of the empire (Lee 1993: 2; 33–4). And all this took place along the same communication lines.

Janni (1984) introduced a distinction between hodological space (from the Greek word *hodos*, meaning path) and cartographic space. The first is linear and mono-dimensional, and corresponds to the concatenations seen in the *itineraria*; the second would produce a three-dimensional, Euclidean type of representation of the world that, according to some, 'was, quite simply, conceptually beyond' the Romans (Lee 1993: 86; see also Salway 2001: 29). For the ancient travellers, who proceeded walking or riding, progressing across a territory was indeed a matter of following secure lines (cf. Geus 2014). Cartography instils an abstraction in the modern eye that distances us from the practical issues of the ancient travellers: a perfectly proportioned representation of a plain on a scale map would not help, if the plain was an impassable marsh.

This said, at the highest levels of the empire's administration all this linear information (or at least a selection of the most important tracts) did converge into the same hands, and was from time to time systematised into general sketch maps: the Map of Agrippa and the *Tabula Peutingeriana* are two examples. They should be considered as updated collections of geographical information in the shape of drawings, with a marked political meaning (cf. Talbert 2010: 142–4); any attempt to extract from them precise physical and chronological information is likely to fail, as providing this information was not their purpose.

Rome combined land and sea travels into a single system, which may be defined as consisting of mono-dimensional and yet pervasive lines, like a gigantic web. The areas of active seafaring of the earlier period along the friendly coasts of the Eastern and Northern Mediterranean were incorporated into a network of maritime lines across the Mediterranean, connected to major thoroughfares that ran on land (see above figure 4.4; cf. Broodbank 2013: 597, figure 11.1; see also Doukellis 2009 and Rathbone 2009). This network of communications had a practical as well as a symbolic role, as it created physical contacts among micro-regions, as well as social relations (Horden and Purcell 2000: 128; cf. Bintliff 2010: 37–9).

The aggregating element of the Roman Empire, therefore, did not lie in an environmental uniformity as happened in Egypt, nor in the possibility to endlessly replicate the same micro-pattern as happened in the Greek world: it consisted of its efficient network of connections, that bridged over gaps, distances, and differences and allowed the spread of the unifying elements that eventually defined the edges of the Roman rule.

Bibliographical references

Primary sources

Ambrose, *Expositio psalmi*. English translation from Salway B. 2001. 'Travel, *itineraria* and *tabellaria*', in C. Adams and R. Laurence (eds.) *Travel and Geography in the Roman Empire*. London/New York, Routledge: 22–66.

Caes., *BCiv*.: Caesar, *De Bello Civili*. English translation from the Perseus Digital Library (perseus.tufts.edu).

Caes., *BGall*.: Caesar, *De Bello Gallico*. English translation from the Perseus Digital Library (perseus.tufts.edu).

Hdt.: Herodotus, *Historiae*. English translation from the Perseus Digital Library (perseus .tufts . edu).

Liv. *Ab urbe cond*.: Titus Livius, *Ab urbe condita*. English translation from the Perseus Digital Library (perseus.tufts.edu).

Plut., *C. Gracc*.: Plutarchus, *Vitae Paralleale, Caius Gracchus*. English translation from the Perseus Digital Library (perseus.tufts.edu).

Polyb.: Polybius, *Historiae*. English translation from the Perseus Digital Library (perseus.tufts.edu).

Str.: Strabo, *Geographia*. English translation from the Perseus Digital Library (perseus .tufts . edu).

Suet., *Aug*.: Suetonius, *Divus Augustus*. English translation from Kolb A. 2001. 'Transport and Communication in the Roman State. The *cursus publicus*', in Adams C. and Laurence R. (eds.), *Travel and Geography in the Roman Empire*. London/New York, Routledge: 95–105.

Veg. *Mil*.: Vegetius, *De re militari*. English translation from the Internet Archive (archive.org).

Secondary sources

Adam J.-P. 2001. *Roman Building: Materials and Techniques*. London/New York, Routledge.

Adams C. 2007. *Land Transport in Roman Egypt: A Study of Economics and Administration in a Roman Province*. Oxford, Oxford University Press.

Austin N. J. E. and Rankov N. B. 1995. *Exploratio: Military and Political Intelligence in the Roman World from the Second Punic War to the Battle of Adrianople*. London/New York, Routledge.

Bintliff J. L. 2010. 'Classical Greek Urbanism: A Social Darwinian View', in R. M. Rosen and I. Sluiter (eds.), *Valuing Others in Classical Antiquity*. Mnemosyne Supplement 323. Leiden/Boston, Brill.

Brodersen K. 2001. 'The Presentation of the Geographical Knowledge for Travel and Transportation in the Roman World', in C. Adams and R. Laurence (eds.), *Travel and Geography in the Roman Empire*. London/New York, Routledge: 7–21.

Broodbank C. 2013. *The Making of the Middle Sea: A History of the Mediterranean from the Beginning to the Emergence of the Classical World*. London, Thames and Hudson.

Brughmans T., Collar A. and Coward F. 2016. *The Connected Past*. Oxford, Oxford University Press.

Carreras C. and De Soto P. 2013. 'The Roman Transport Network: A Precedent for the Integration of the European Mobility', *Historical Methods: A Journal of Quantitative and Interdisciplinary History* 46.3: 117–33.

Casson L. 1994. *Travel in the Ancient World*. Baltimore/London, Johns Hopkins University Press.

Clarke K. 1999. *Between Geography and History: Hellenistic Constructions of the Roman World*. Oxford Classical Monographs. Oxford, Clarendon Press.

Cuomo S. 2001. *Ancient Mathematics*. London/New York, Routledge.

Cuomo S. 2007. *Technology and Culture in Greek and Roman Antiquity*. Cambridge, Cambridge University Press.

Dalgaard C.-J., Kaarsen N., Olsson O. and Selaya P. 2018. 'Roman Roads to Prosperity: Persistence and Non-Persistence of Public Goods Provision', *CEPR Discussion Paper* DP12745.

Dan A., Crom W., Geus K., Görz G., Guckelsberger K., König V., Poiss T. and Thiering M. 2016. 'Common Sense Geography and Ancient Geographical Texts', *Journal for Ancient Studies*, Special Volume 6 - Space and Knowledge: 571–97.

Davidson J. 1991. 'The Gaze in Polybius' Histories', *Journal of Roman Studies* 81: 10–24.

Dilke O. A. W. 1987a. 'Maps in the Service of the State: Roman Cartography to the End of the Augustan Era', in J. B. Harley and D. Woodward (eds.), *History of Cartography*, vol. 1. Chicago, University of Chicago Press, chapter 12: 201–11.

Dilke O. A. W. 1987b. 'Roman Large-Scale Mapping in the Early Empire', in J. B. Harley and D. Woodward (eds.), *History of Cartography*, vol. 1. Chicago, University of Chicago Press, chapter 12: 212–33.

Dilke O. A. W. 1987c. 'Itineraries and Geographical Maps in the Early and Late Roman Empires', in J. B. Harley and D. Woodward (eds.), *History of Cartography*, vol. 1. Chicago, University of Chicago Press, chapter 12: 213–57.

Dilke O. A. W., Harley J. B. and Woodward D. 1987. 'The Culmination of Greek Cartography in Ptolemy', in J. B. Harley and D. Woodward (eds.), *History of Cartography*, vol. 1. Chicago, University of Chicago Press, chapter 11: 177–200.

Doukellis P. N. 2009. 'Hadrian's Panhellenion: A Network of Cities?', in I. Malkin, C. Costantakopoulou and K. Panagopoulou (eds.), *Greek and Roman Networks in the Mediterranean*. London/New York, Routledge: 285–98.

Elton H. 1996. *Frontiers of the Roman Empire*. London, Batsford.

Geus K. 2014. 'L'influenza delle condizioni geo-fisiche sulla mobilità nel Mar Rosso nell'età antica', *Sileno* 40: 109–22.

Goldsworthy A. 2000. *Roman Warfare*. London, Cassell.

Goldsworthy A. 2003. *The Complete Roman Army*. London, Thames and Hudson.

Güimil-Fariña A. and Parcero-Oubiña C. 2015. '"Dotting the Joins": A Non-Reconstructive Use of Least Cost Paths to Approach Ancient Roads: The Case of the Roman Roads in the NW Iberian Peninsula', *Journal of Archaeological Science* 54: 31–44.

Hanson V. D. (ed.) 2010. *Makers of Ancient Strategy: From the Persian Wars to the Fall of Rome*. Princeton/Oxford, Princeton University Press.

Harley J. B., Woodward D. and Aujac J. 1987. 'Greek Cartography in the Early Roman World', in J. B. Harley and D. Woodward (eds.), *History of Cartography*, vol. 1. Chicago, University of Chicago Press, chapter 10: 161–76.

Hitchner B. R. 2012. 'Roads, Integration, Connectivity, and Economic Performance in the Roman Empire', in S. E. Alcock, J. Bodel, and R. J. A. Talbert (eds.), *Highways, Byways, and Road Systems in the Pre-Modern World*. Malden, John Wiley & Sons: 222–34.

Horden P. and Purcell N. 2000. *The Corrupting Sea: A Study of the Mediterranean History*. Malden/Oxford/Carlton, Blackwell Publishing.

Janni P. 1984. *La mappa e il periplo: Cartografia antica e spazio odologico*. Roma, Bretschneider.

Kehne P. 2007. 'War- and Peacetime Logistics: Supplying Imperial Armies in East and West', in P. Erdkamp (ed.), *A Companion to the Roman Army*. Chichester, Wiley-Blackwell: 323–38.

Kennedy D. and Riley D. 1990. *Rome's Desert Frontier from the Air*. Austin, University of Texas Press.

Kolb A. 2001. 'Transport and Communication in the Roman State: The *cursus publicus*', in C. Adams and R. Laurence (eds.), *Travel and Geography in the Roman Empire*. London/New York, Routledge: 95–105.

Lee A. D. 1993. *Information & Frontiers: Roman Foreign Relations in Late Antiquity*. Cambridge, Cambridge University Press.

Lolos Y. 2009. 'Via Egnatia after Egnatius: Imperial Policy and Inter-Regional Contacts', in I. Malkin, C. Costantakopoulou and K. Panagopoulou (eds.), *Greek and Roman Networks in the Mediterranean*. London/New York, Routledge: 264–84.

Luttwak E. N. 1999. *The Grand Strategy of the Roman Empire*. London, Weidenfeld Nicholson.

Mackay Ch. 2004. *Ancient Rome: A Military and Political History*. Cambridge, Cambridge University Press.

Mattingly D. J. 2011. *Imperialism, Power and Identity: Experiencing the Roman Empire*. Princeton/Oxford, Princeton University Press.

Mayerson P. 1996. 'The Port of Clysma (Suez) in Transition from Roman to Arab Rule', *Journal of Near Eastern Studies* 55.2: 119–26.

Nicolet C. 1991. *Space, Geography, and Politics in the Early Roman Empire*. Ann Arbor, University of Michigan Press.

Parker P. 2010. *The Empire Stops Here: A Journey along the Frontiers of the Roman World*. London, Pimlico.

Rathbone D. 2009. 'Merchant Networks in the Greek World: The Impact of Rome', in I. Malkin, C. Costantakopoulou and K. Panagopoulou (eds.), *Greek and Roman Networks in the Mediterranean*. London/New York, Routledge: 299–310.

Salway B. 2001. 'Travel, *itineraria* and *tabellaria*', in C. Adams and R. Laurence (eds.), *Travel and Geography in the Roman Empire*. London/New York, Routledge: 22–66.

Scarre C. 1995. *The Penguin Historical Atlas of Ancient Rome*. London, Penguin.
Sheehan P., Karelin D., Karelina M. and Zhitpeleva T. 2018. 'Reconstruction of the Diocletianic Fortress in Babylon of Egypt: Sources and Reconstruction Argumentation', in *Virtual Archaeology (from Air, on Earth, under Water and at Museum), Proceedings of the International Forum held at the State Hermitage Museum 28–30 May 2018*. Saint Petersburg, The Hermitage State Publishers: 224–33.
Sidebotham S. S., Hense M. and Nouwens H. M. 2008. *The Red Land: The Illustrated Archaeology of Egypt's Eastern Desert*. Cairo/New York, the American University in Cairo Press.
Southern P. 1990. 'Signals versus Illumination on Roman Frontiers', *Britannia* 21: 233–42.
Southern P. 2001. *The Roman Empire from Severus to Constantine*. London/New York, Routledge.
Southern P. and Dixon K.R. 1996. *The Late Roman Army*. London, Routledge.
Strobel K. 2001. 'Strategy and Army Structure between Septimius Severus and Constantine the Great', in P. Erdkamp (ed.), *A Companion to the Roman Army*. Chichester, Wiley-Blackwell: 266–85.
Talbert R. J. A. 2010. *Rome's World: The Peutinger Map Reconsidered*. Cambridge, Cambridge University Press.
Talbert R. J. A. 2012. 'Urbs Roma to Orbis Romanus', in R. J. A. Talbert (ed.), *Ancient Perspectives: Maps and Their Places in Mesopotamia, Egypt, Greece and Rome*. Chicago, University of Chicago Press, 170–2.
Tierney J. J. 1962–1964. 'The Map of Agrippa', *Proceedings of the Royal Irish Academy: Archaeology, Culture, History, Literature* 63: 151–66.
Van der Heyden A. A. M. and Scullard H. H. 1963. *Atlas of the Classical World*. London, Nelson.
Walbank F. W. 1943. 'Polybius on the Roman Constitution', *The Classical Quarterly* 37.3/4: 73–89.
Wells P. S. 1999. *The Barbarians Speak: How the Conquered Peoples Shaped Roman Europe*. Princeton/Oxford, Princeton University Press.
Whately C. 2015. 'Making Sense of the Frontier Army in the Late Antiquity: An Historian's Perspective', in R. Collins, M. Symonds and M. Weber (eds.), *Roman Military Architecture on the Frontiers*. Oxford/Philadelphia, Oxbow Books: 6–17.
Wheeler E. L. 2011. 'The Army and the Limes in the East', in P. Erdkamp (ed.), *A Companion to the Roman Army*. Chichester, Wiley-Blackwell: 235–66.
Whittaker C. R. 2004. *Rome and its Frontiers: The Dynamics of Empire*. London/New York, Routledge.

5 Recontextualisations

Everyone supposes that 'things that are' are somewhere, because 'what is not' is nowhere (Arist., Ph. 208a29-31).

Transmissions

Appropriation of space and places

Information and objects moved together with people. In Antiquity, travelling for leisure was not uncommon among those who could afford it, but most of the movements took place for commercial reasons, and to engage in warfare. These two reasons mights be also mixed, of course, as new territories were targeted for their resources and the opportunities that they offered.

Trade and military campaigns represented the most obvious occasions to get to know new, vast territories: this holds for Alexander the Great and his conquest of Persia that went on to include the exploration of western India in the IV century BCE (Harley, Woodward and Aujac 1987b: 149), as well as, twenty-two centuries later, for Napoleon and his campaign in Egypt against the British, during which the group of *savants* that he took with him collected enough information to fill in the monumental *Description de l'Égypte*, which took twenty years to be published.

In particular, military campaigns represented, and still represent (cf. Hanson 2010), the most obvious case in which the knowledge of the territory and the ability to organise the movements of people and goods across it make the difference between success and disaster, and between life and death. The weight and importance of these two elements grow as the fighters leave their original territories and move to unfamiliar grounds. If the Egyptians rarely fought in totally alien environments, the Persians, who did try to conquer unfamiliar lands, paid a high price: Cambyses lost his army somewhere in Egypt's Western Desert, and Darius' and Xerxes' attempts to conquer the Aegean failed due to the necessity to squeeze and manoeuvre their large armies into the meandering Greek territory and coasts. In this respect, a winning asset of the Roman empire was the careful planning and organisation that made the army a flexible and adaptable force, able to fight always in the same way in totally different environments, thus appearing to be virtually unstoppable.

The organisation of wars and battles requests specific logistic arrangements that might, or might not, reflect the normal travel and trade arrangements during peaceful times. More generally, they might or might not correspond to already experienced ways of dealing with space and places. Most of the wars fought by the Egyptians, for instance, took place along the Nile, either to re-unite the country or to add further portions of valley to the territory under their direct control. The Middle Kingdom king Senusret III launched a devastating campaign to subdue Nubia (cf. Figure 2.2) and, on his way back, left behind an inscription engraved in stone:

'I have made my boundary further south than my fathers, I have added to what was bequeathed to me. I am a king who speaks and acts, what my heart plans is done by my arm. One who attacks to conquer, who is swift to succeed, in whose heart a plan does not slumber. (…) Attack is valour, retreat is cowardice. A coward is he who is driven from his border' (boundary stele of Semna 4-10).

Middle Kingdom troops moved along the Nile by boat, then disembarked and fought on land. The same system is likely to have been adopted by the southern king Kamose, who re-united the country, split in two parts when the Hyksos had conquered the norther portion during the Second Intermediate Period. From Thebes, Kamose boldly sailed northwards directly to Avaris, the Hyksos capital located in the Delta, passing by all the other cities and settlements along the river that were controlled by the Hyksos and lay siege to the city (Spalinger 2005: 3).

Once the country was re-united, the powerful New Kingdom pharaohs turned their attention towards Palestine and Syria, which meant, however, getting ready to fight in a different situation: the dry conditions of the land were similar, but the absence of the river made a significant difference. The Egyptian army underwent a profound re-organisation in the subsequent decades, and by the time of Tuthmosis I the navy was no longer called 'the royal army': the land-based army, based on the use of chariots and relying on different travelling arrangements, became the main military force (Spalinger 2005: 6 and 32-9). This new organisation allowed Tuthmosis III and later Ramses II to expand all the way to Megiddo and then Qadesh, in modern Syria, where important battles were fought. Once this historical period characterised by stability and strong centralised power ended, the

118 *Recontextualisations*

same happened to far-reaching military enterprises in foreign and relatively alien territories, and the country retired back within its usual boundaries, with small variations over the time. Of course, trading and exploratory expeditions pre-date and continued well after the New Kingdom attempts to expand the lands under direct Egyptian rule (Creasman and Wilkinson 2017) and their development is by no means in contrast with a territorial stability.

Apart from the specific case of Athens, Greek *poleis* generally fought, individually or as allied groups, to defend or gain influence on other similarly organised entities. As we have seen above, they fought all together as a single 'country' only to defend themselves against the Persian invasions (cf. Figure 3.4). The Greek galaxy always remained a collection of separated places concentrated in a specific region, but potentially able to endlessly expand in the space, by multiplying themselves whenever and wherever another suitable place was found.

In the case of Rome, which expanded over significantly different territories and environments (cf. Figure 4.1), exploration, construction of infrastructures and military campaigns become deeply entangled, and all belonged to the same intention to expand the Roman control over the known world (Dilke, Harley and Woodward 1987: 178). It is interesting to note that the movement of troops across hostile territories during aggressive military campaigns implied the construction, every evening, of a marching camp based always on the same layout, that acted as 'a powerful psychological device. For troops venturing into hostile territory and possibly exotic surroundings, the familiar context of the camp defences would provide a welcome sense of security' (Luttwak 1999: 56). They basically re-created every evening a familiar place, an action that supported and facilitated the process of appropriation of the foreign land.

Lines of penetration into foreign territories were used not only to reach a final destination, but also to transport and transfer along them a way to perceive, describe and organize an unexplored space, and turn it into a familiar place (cf. Figure 4.4). In fact, military campaigns generally represented a first phase of aggression meant to establish a firm control on the territory, and the same infrastructures were later used to implement state-controlled travel and trade, as well as to allow the development of short- and medium-range movements of the local populations.

In Antiquity, the geometric appropriation and control of the space worked well to a small scale, where it had a number of practical applications. The Roman *centuriatio*, the layout of aqueducts, the construction of tunnels were all based on superimposing a spatial grid or a network of reference points on the various places. When the scale of the movements grew, the same happened to the approximation of the numerical measurements. At the administrative level, this lack of precision might be relatively unimportant in the realm of propaganda, but was instead crucial when planning strategic movements across the empire. From a certain point onwards, space was not sufficient any longer to measure distances: time could represent a more reliable indication. This could be due to a lack of precise information on the distances (cf. Geus 2012), or on the fact that longer journeys were more likely to be affected by unexpected obstacles or unpredictable events. Even today, whoever travels by car in the sandy desert knows very well that distances are better measured in terms of time than in terms of kilometres, as a field of dunes can take hours to be passed over or circumnavigated, and the same route might take a shorter or a longer time depending on the temperature of the sand.

Objects and ideas on the move

Movements across land and seas transferred people, objects and a varying amount of cultural baggage. Objects might change function or meaning in their new location, thus introducing an additional twist in their biography (cf. Greco 2019). Some objects (and relating technologies) were traded in mass for their daily use, others instead were imported as unique or rare specimens, as a demonstration of the power to reach distant and exotic lands (cf. Mark 2017 and Shaw 2017). Whilst the meaning of written documents communicating straightforward information (such as lists of items or orders) remained mostly unchanged between their departure and their arrival point, it is difficult to establish if and how the cultural background of objects was filtered or modified once they reached distant lands (cf. Osborne 2009).

Even more difficult is to trace what happened to stories and ideas: as with objects, once transferred into a different physical and cultural environment they might or might not retain their original meaning and function. In the first case, they would act as reminders of their original context, as the 'classic' Homeric passages found on the walls of the Late Roman houses in the Dakhla Oasis, at the southern outskirts of the Roman empire in Egypt's Western Desert (McFadden 2019). In the second case, instead, they might transform and take a different role, suggested by or exploiting their new location. A significant example of this second case is the Temple of Isis at Beneventum, a small town located in the interland of Campania, in southern Italy. There the cult of the Egyptian goddess was promoted by the Flavii, keen on exhibiting a divine origin of their power; in particular, the emperor Domitian, who wished to be acknowledged as *dominus et deus*, found convenient to represent himself as a pharaoh in an Egyptian-style statue and to pair himself with Horus, son of Isis (Bülow-Clausen 2012; Pirelli 2007; Müller 1969).

The cult of Isis had reached Beneventum before the Flavii along the trade routes via Puteoli and Pompeii. Beneventum itself was located at the junction of the *Via Appia* and the *Via Latina* and owed its fortune in Roman times to its strategic position: in the *Tabula Peutingeriana* it is represented as the nodal point from where five roads depart, and the *Itinerarium Antonini* provides distances to and from Beneventum and important harbours on the Tyrrhenian and on the Ionian Sea. The presence there of a statue of a Roman emperor dressed as a pharaoh acted as a clear message to the persistent flow of long-distance travellers passing through Beneventum on their way to or from the oriental provinces of the empire, who would be able to catch the underlying meaning: the Roman rule moved along those roads and spread as a pervasive tide in all directions; and all this happened thanks to the people who walked and rode along them, day after day, year after year.

History, space, and places

Three ways

To summarise, ancient Egypt, Greece and Rome evolved in three different geographical contexts, each determining and inspiring different internal and external interactions.

Ancient Egypt's culture cannot be disjoined from its specific environment: it was defined by its land and its annual rhythm, and its identity was so deeply rooted in its territory that it represented a model that could not be exported. It might expand, as it did, along the Nile, where the geographic conditions were basically the same: the Nubian region, in modern Sudan, was for centuries either heavily influenced or militarily conquered by its powerful neighbours rooted downstream. Any attempt to expand the Egyptian direct rule beyond the environment of the Nile Valley and permanently incorporate different territories lasted instead a relatively short time (cf. Figures 2.2 and 2.3).

Ancient Egyptian time moved along circles (the inundation and the kings' reigns) and along a line (the uninterrupted replication of the same order, cf. Pinch 2002: 57). For about twenty centuries, this system also corresponded to an independent and powerful state, which survived several threats to its unity and integrity; for the ten subsequent centuries it managed to retain its cultural memory, even if absorbed into the complex dynamics of the Mediterranean world. The balance of this system rested on the idea that being whole and united was the natural state of the Nilotic population, and that any attempt to break it would have been countered by centripetal forces, including the strong common identity and the necessity to coordinate the efforts to better dominate the inundation. This was especially true, of course, from the perspective of a ruling house eager to maintain (and re-gain, if necessary) the full control of a fertile and productive territory.

The ancient Greek world can be instead described as a network of inter-dependent dots, which was able to expand to surprising lengths along lines across the sea – or, better – along its coasts (cf Figures 3.3 and 3.5). Even if separated by miles of water, originating from different areas, implementing shifting agendas, all these dots did belong to a single system that accumulated and exchanged information and knowledge, and achieved significant results in terms of comprehension of the known world, ranging from the exploration of extremely distant lands to the calculation of the circumference of the Earth. They never joined together to create larger and stable entities, but multiplied whenever the environmental conditions allowed to replicate the same scheme, that is, whenever there was a safe harbour, sufficient water and a productive patch of land.

The Roman rule can be described as a pervasive and yet flexible system, based on lines of communication. The focus on mobility and the ability to build a network of efficient routes allowed Rome to quickly absorb different geographic environments together with the different cultures that populated them. The Romans, in a way, combined the large-scale control that was typical of ancient Egypt (but without strictly linking it to a single environment and to a single culture) with the connectivity that was typical of the Greek galaxy (but expanding it on land as never before). Whereas Greeks and Carthaginians had ruled over the coasts and Alexander the Great, even if briefly, over land, Rome ruled over both, and to a geographical and chronological extent never reached before (cf. Broodbank 2013: 606, figure 11.2).

The perception of limit changed from one system to the other. The Egyptian distrust for the sea depended on the fact that the 'the Great Green' represented a different environment altogether from the one in which they usually moved. For the Greek, the Pillars of Herakles represented the limit of their direct knowledge; in this respect, there was a strict correlation between physical and mental limits. The combination of fear and fascination of the unknown is embodied by one of the most significant ancient Greek figures, Odysseus: in fact, in the XIII century, the Italian poet Dante imagined that he eventually died after he crossed the Pillars of Herakles in an insane attempt to surpass the established limits. All this anxiety for the unknown does not seem to have affected the Romans: the maximum extent of the empire was reached thanks to the combination of two factors: the presence, in most areas, of natural boundaries that could be managed in a relatively easy way (sea, rivers and deserts), and the ability to maintain efficient communications within this vast and heterogeneous territory (cf. Figures 4.3 and 4.4).

Three different original territorial contexts shaped three different modalities of interaction with the surrounding world. Three different perceptions and descriptions of the surrounding world (*geo-graphia*) shaped plans and decisions of the people who lived there and then, and thus the historical events that, literally, 'took place' there. Egypt, Greece and Rome are just three examples, of course: there are certainly more, both from the ancient and from the modern world (e.g. Scardigno 2018). The 'description of the Earth' of modern city-dwellers who travel by train and plane is based on territorial landmarks and reference points that are completely different from those of people who lived, or still live, surrounded by more incumbent and less filtered environments.

Forma mentis

As Casey noted, 'we are emplaced beings, to begin with' (1997: x). In Antiquity, the role of place was explicitly discussed by Greek philosophers, in particular Aristoteles, for whom 'where something is' constituted a basic metaphysical category, together with substance, quantity, quality, relativity, time, attitude, state, action and affection (Casey 1997: 50). He paired the place to a vessel, surrounding its content and giving it a shape (Arist., *Ph.* 209b3-6); the verb used to describe what the vessel does is *periechein*, literally to hold (*echein*) around (*peri*). However, as a vessel can move whereas place must be unmovable (*akineton*), he went on to define a place as 'the first unchangeable limit of that-which-surrounds (*tou periechontos*)' (Arist., *Ph.* 212a20-21).

Movement and place are strictly related and interdependent, as 'the existence of place (*topos*) is made clear by the exchange of position (*antimetastasis*)' (Arist., *Ph.* 208b1-2). The word for movement used by Artistotle is *phora*, that appears also in Plato to indicate a movement of translation, vs. *kinesis* meaning (com)motion (Pl., *Tht.* 152d). The place described as a limit, articulated in the four dimensions of space and time, shapes the human actions just like the vessel shapes the liquid, or the unmovable limit 'holds around' it contents. Our attempt to describe the appearance of this limit is our *geo-graphia*, and our transfers within it, at the same time, define and are defined by it.

The physical context in which we live and move shapes our movements and thus our actions, the objects that we produce and use, and the choices that we make; in other words, it shapes our *forma mentis*. And *viceversa*, of course: we create, find or modify places to suit our needs and expectations. This happens in physical, but also in metaphysical terms: all the creations myths include, and many actually coincide with the creation of a place – actually of two places (land/water, earth/heaven), as one can only be defined

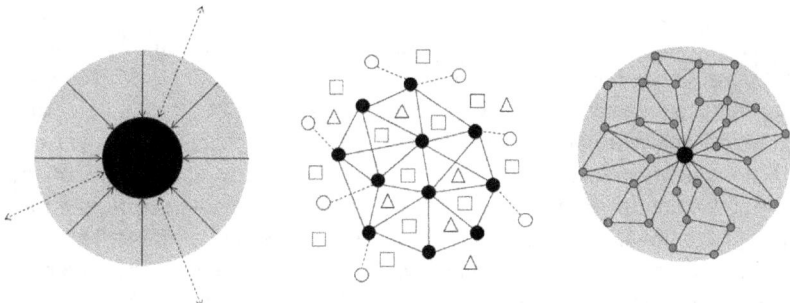

Figure 5.1 Mega-place, para-place, and meta-place.

if compared to something else (Casey 1997: 8, 12). Places are thus deeply related to our *forma mentis*, in all the various senses of the word *forma*: shape, contour, figure, outline, appearance, stamp and, why not, map as well. Our 'mental map' is a mirror image of our *geo-graphia*.

The Egyptian, Greek and Roman cultures were born and evolved in three different places. Egypt was immersed in its own mega-place, which was stable, rooted, global, comprehensive and environing. The Greek galaxy developed (in) a para-place, a network constructed by finding and connecting places with similar characteristics, that is, by emplacing the same model in extremely similar contexts. The Roman empire constructed instead a meta-place, a system of connections that allowed the spread of fixed and yet flexible elements, pervasive because able to transcend contingencies (Figure 5.1).

The movements inspired and encouraged by the mega-place are strongly centripetal (in Egypt, everything converged to the Nile Valley). They are accompanied, and partly balanced, by linear tentacles that stretch outwards in specific directions (long-ranging commercial or military expeditions), and that can be cut off or abandoned if the resources to maintain them become insufficient (e.g. transregional caravan routes and Nubian and Middle Eastern territories, conquered in periods of strong power and then abandoned). In mega-places *kinesis* (commotion) is frowned upon and *phora* (translation) takes place mainly within its boundaries. A mega-place is self-contained and focussed on itself, and the people who inhabit it spend considerable time and efforts to maintain the *status quo* (in Egypt, most of the population was permanently dedicated to the agricultural exploitation of the annual inundation).

A para-place, by definition, consists of a network of similar points (e.g. the Greek cities). The movements taking place among them are an integral part of this system; actually, the relationship between points and movements may be paired to the egg-chicken dilemma. Para-places are founded on the overall concept of *phora* (the translations exploiting the connectivity along the coasts) that might be triggered by local or individual *kinesis* (commotions due to the excessive growth of the population or the need of new land).

Within a meta-place (like the Roman Empire), establishing a network of movements is instrumental to spread a few, precise and non-negotiable principles defining a global identity (the administrative structure, the trading system, the organisation of the army, the Roman citizenship). Therefore *phora* is crucial (the translation of people and information must efficiently take place along the road network), and *kinesis* (the commotion due, for instance, to raids along the borders, but also to the persistence of local beliefs and habits) is tolerated until it threatens to disrupt the essential *phora* that allowed the global system to work.

A mega-place has an interior and an exterior, is an entity with a precise identity surrounded by the rest of the world. A para-place can reproduce itself endlessly, provided that the environmental conditions are the same. In this respect, it corresponds to a network of places scattered in the space, but rooted in the same specific environment; its exterior is represented by all the other environmental conditions, that do not favour its reproduction. A meta-place exists thanks to a few, encompassing principles that are able to link different environments just because they are not dependent on them. A meta-place can stretch for as long as its internal connectivity allows to maintain these links.

These simplified models may be thus used to describe and analyse the ancient Egyptian, Greek and Roman civilisations, and might be also applied to other similar cases. My knowledge stops here, but the potential of this approach does not: the identification, construction and adoption of models of the same type, but applied to completely different situations, may offer the chance to reveal patterns, similarities and differences in how we experienced and experience the world that surrounds us. These would, in turn, add a further layer to our knowledge of history and our comprehension of how the past shaped our present. After all, it is always a matter of context.

Bibliographical references

Primary sources

Arist., *Ph.*: Aristoteles, *Physica*. English translation from the Internet Archive (archive.org).
Boundary stele of Senusret III at Semna. English translation from Lichtheim M. 1973. *Ancient Egyptian Literature. Vol. I: The Old and Middle Kingdoms*. Berkley/Los Angeles/London: University of California Press: 118–20.

Pl., *Tht.*: Plato, *Theaetetus*. English translation from the Perseus Digital Library (perseus .tufts . edu).

Secondary sources

Broodbank C. 2013. *The Making of the Middle Sea: A History of the Mediterranean from the Beginning to the Emergence of the Classical World*. London, Thames and Hudson.

Bülow-Clausen K. 2012. 'Domitian between Isis and Minerva: The Dialogue between the "Egyptian" and "Graeco-Roman" Aspects of the Sanctuary of Isis at Beneventum', *Supplement to MYTHOS* 3: 93–122.

Casey E. S. 1997. *The Fate of Place: A Philosophical History*. Berkeley/Los Angeles/London, University of California Press.

Creasman P. P. and Wilkinson R. H. 2017. *Pharaoh's Land and Beyond*. Oxford, Oxford University Press.

Dilke O. A. W., Harley J. B. and Woodward D. 1987. 'The Culmination of Greek Cartography in Ptolemy', in J. B. Harley and D. Woodward (eds.), *History of Cartography*, vol. 1. Chicago, University of Chicago Press, chapter 11: 177–200.

Geus K. 2012. 'A Day's Journey in Herodotus' Histories', in K. Geus and M. Thiering (eds.), *Common Sense Geography and Mental Modelling*. Berlin, Max Planck Institute for the History of Science, MPIWG Preprint 426: 110–8.

Greco C. 2019. 'The Biography of Objects', *The International Archives of the Photogrammetry, Remote Sensing and Spatial Information Sciences* XLII-2/ W11: 5–10.

Hanson V. D.(ed.) 2010. *Makers of Ancient Strategy: From the Persian Wars to the Fall of Rome*. Princeton/Oxford, Princeton University Press.

Harley J. B., Woodward D. and Aujac J. 1987. 'The Growth of an Empirical Cartography in Hellenistic Greece', in J. B. Harley and D. Woodward (eds.), *History of Cartography*, vol. 1. Chicago, University of Chicago Press, chapter 9: 148–60.

Lichtheim M. 1973. *Ancient Egyptian Literature. Vol. I: The Old and Middle Kingdoms*. Berkley/Los Angeles/London, University of California Press.

Luttwak E. N. 1999. *The Grand Strategy of the Roman Empire*. London, Weidenfeld Nicholson.

Mark S. 2017. 'The Long Arm of Merchantry: Trade Interactions', in P. P. Creasman and R. H. Wilkinson (eds.), *Pharaoh's Land and Beyond*. Oxford, Oxford University Press: 115–31.

McFadden S. 2019. 'Wall Painting in the Western Oases', in R. S. Bagnall and G. Tallet (eds.), *The Great Oasis of Egypt: The Kharga and Dakhla Oases in Antiquity*. Cambridge, Cambridge University Press: 281–96.

Müller H. W. 1969. *Der Isiskult im antiken Benevent und Katalog der Skulpturen aus den ägyptischen Heiligtümern im Museo del Sannio zu Benevent*. Berlin, Hessling.

Osborne R. 2009. 'What Travelled with Greek Pottery?', in I. Malkin, C. Costantakopoulou and K. Panagopoulou (eds.), *Greek and Roman Networks in the Mediterranean*. London/New York, Routledge: 83–93.

Pinch G. 2002. *Egyptian Mythology: A Guide to the Gods, Goddesses, and Traditions of Ancient Egypt*. Oxford, Oxford University Press.

Pirelli R. 2007. 'Il culto di Iside a Benevento', in I. Bragantini, R. Pirelli and I. Incordino (eds.), *Il culto di Iside a Benevento*. Napoli, Electa: 9–17.

Scardigno N. 2018. *Landscape as Forma Mentis: Interpreting the Integral Dimension of the Anthropic Space. Mongolia*. Milano, Franco Angeli.

Shaw I. 2017. 'Technology in Transit: The Borrowing of Ideas in Science and Craftwork', in P. P. Creasman and R. H. Wilkinson (eds.), *Pharaoh's Land and Beyond*. Oxford, Oxford University Press: 167–80.

Spalinger A. J. 2005. *War in Ancient Egypt: The New Kingdom*. Malden/Oxford/Victoria, Blackwell.

Index

Adriatic Sea 98, 110
Aegean Sea 15, 19, 56, 61, 68, *72*, 116
Africa 19, 31, 39, 41, 73, 79, 80, 90, 104
Akhenaten 35–36, 43
Alexander the Great 17, 68, 91, 116, 121
Alexandria 7, 8, 103
Almásy, László 14
Amduat xi, 36
Antonine Wall 97
apoikia 77, 81
aqueduct 1, 4, 103, 118
Aristoteles 9, 11, 57, 61, 77, 122
Asia xi, 10, 74, 77; Asia Minor 56, 64, 68, 76
Aswan 7, 27, 31, 40; dam 31–32, 39
Athens 57, 61–62, 66–68, 71, 74, 77, 104, 118
Augustus 95, 100, 104

barbarians 68, 73, 77
Beneventum 119–20
Black Sea 56, 71, 81
boat 18, 19, 28, 38–39, 48, 70, 107, 117
bridge 2, 3, 9, 66, 67, 87, 91, 96, 100, 103, 106
Britain 20, 79, 80, 89, 97

Caesar 87, 89, 96, 106–7, 110
camel 14–15, 40, 108
car 1, 14–15, 119
caravan route 31, 123
Carthage 54, 74, 79, 81, 90, 110, 121
cartography 8, 12, 14, 103–4, 111

centuriatio 103, 118
city 35, 44, 54, *58*, *60*, 63, 77–78, 90–91, 106, 109, 117; city-state 15, 56–57, 61–62, 64, 68
Claudios Ptolemaios 8, 13, 18–19, 103–5
climate 9–11, 33, 55, 69
colonialism 11
colonization 77, 81
colony 54, 56, *60*, 63, *65*, 77–81, 90
connectivity 69, 70, *72*, 81, 82, 96, 109, 121, 124
Constantinopolis 104, 108
context 2, 5, 11, 22, 118–24
cursus publicus 38, 101, 108

Dakhla Oasis 15, 119
Danube 20, 66, 90, 96, 108
death 17, 46, 68, 90; (concept of) 19, 27, 31, 33–34, 36–37, 47, 116
determinism 11
Diocletian 89, 108–9
donkey 15, 18, 19, 40–41

earth 6, 7, 9, 12–14, 18–19, 31, 34, 41, 46, 47, 58, 74, 81, 103–5, 121–22
Eastern Desert 3, 27, 31, 34, 41, 100, 105, 108
Egypt xi, 1, 3, 6, 10, 14, 15, 17–20, 27, *28–30*, 31–34, 38, 40, 42–43, 46–48, 54, 64, 68, 74, 78, 80–81, 87, 90, 100, 105, 108, 111, 116, 119–23; Lower Egypt 43–46; Upper Egypt 40, 43–46
emporion 77–78

Index

environment 2, 3, 7, 9–12, 17, 19–20, 31, 33, 37, 40, 48, 56, 69, 74, 80–81, 87, 89, 90, 97, 112, 116–17, 120–22, 124
Eratosthenes 7–9, 76
ethnos 55–56, 62

flood 32–33, 36–39, 42–43, 47; see also inundation
Fossatum Africae 97
frontier 28, 90, 95–97, 108–9

Gaul 87, 89–90, 102–4, 106, 110
geography xii, 4–7, 12, 13, 18, 20, 73; geographical knowledge 8–9, 13, 75
geometry 32, 104
Gibraltar 70, 72
Gilf al-Kebir 15
Giza 39, 42
Google Earth 2, 4, 27, *28*, *57*, 87, *88*
Greece 6–7, 12, 15, 17–18, 32, 54–56, *55*, 63–64, 66–68, 73, 76, 87, 90, 120, 122

Hadrian 97, 109; Hadrian's Wall 97; *Via Hadriana* 108
Hanno 79–80
harbour 10, 39, 70, 78, 120–21
Harkhuf 40–41
Hellenistic Period 7, 8, 17
Herodotos x, 7–10, 32, 62, 64, 66, 67, 73–74, 80, 100
Hierakonpolis 37, 43–45
hieroglyph 15, 32, 34, 38, 47
Himlico 79
Hippodamos 63
history x-xii, 1, 4–8, 11, 14–15, 18–20, 27–28, 32, 44, 64, 69, 76, 95, 120, 124
Homer 69, 74; Homeric poem 73, 75, 119
horizon 34–35, 48, 76
Horus 34, 44–46, 119

identity xi, 18, 20, 55, 57, 61, 68, 78, 120, 124
imperialism 11, 95
India 68, 116
inundation 19, 31–34, 36, 38–39, 42–43, 120, 123; see also flood
Ionian Sea 15, 61, 71, 79, 120

irrigation 32, 42, 47
Isis 34, 119–20
island xi, 19, 32, 36, 38, 54, 56, 62, 67–71, *72*, 75–76, 78, 81, 91
Italy 1, 10, 56, 71, 78, 87, 90–91, 119
itinerary 13, 20, 38, 40–41, 70, 73, 100–2, 104–5, 111; *Itinerarium Antonini* 99, 102–3, 105, 120

Khufu 34, 38, 42
king list xi, 43, 46

landscape xii, 7, 10, 12, 19–20, 22, 33, 35, 38, 41, 48, 73
Libya 20, 80, 87; Libyan Desert 14
life xi, 3, 10, 12, 14, 19, 31, 33, 48, 61, 89, 100; (concept of) 19, 27, 31, 33–34, 37, 45, 48, 56, 116
limes 108–9

Macedonia 68, 87, 90, 108
map 4, 10, 12–13, *21*, *28*, 40–41, *55*, 69, 73–74, 76, *88*, 95, *99*, 103–5, 110–11, 123
Marathon 64, 66–67
Mediterranean (Sea) 8, 9, 11–12, 17, 19–20, 27–28, 42–43, 57, 61, 63–64, 69–71, 73–74, 76, 79–81, 88, 90–91, 98, 109, 111, 120
memory 20, 22, 106, 120
Mesopotamia 17, 44, 54
Middle Kingdom xi, *29*, 33, 38–39, 43, 117
mummification 34, 39
myth x, xi, 33–34, 45, 78, 122

Narmer 43–45
network 3, 12, 17, 20, 37, 42, 61, 63, 70, 79, 81, 91, 95, 98, 100, 102, 105, 107–11, 118, 121, 123–24
New Kingdom xi, 28, *30*, 34, 117–18
Nile 7, 14, 15, 19, 20, 27, 31, 33–36, 38, 40, 42–44, 48, 80, 117, 120; Nile Delta 28, 43, 117; Nile Valley 19, *29–30*, 31–32, 108, 117, 120, 123
Nilometre 32
Nubia 28, 117, 120, 123

oasis 1, 3, 15, 19, 27, 31, 40, 46, 119
obelisk 37–38, 48

Index

object 2–4, 11, 43, 95, 116, 119, 122
ocean 5, 69, 73–74, 89, 95
Odysseus 75–76, 78
oikoumene 73–74, 103, 110
Old Kingdom *29*, 37, 40–41
orbis terrarium 104, 110
Osiris 34, 36

pack animals 14, 38, 40, 101
Palermo stone 32
periplous 70–71, *72*, 102
Persians 68, 100, 116; army 64, 66, 67, 116; empire 64, *65*, 68, 91; wars x, 64–67, 118
phenomenology 12
Phoenicians 17, 56, *58*, *60*, 74, 79–81
Pillars of Herakles 54, 57, 70, 74, 79–80
place (concept of) x, 2–4, 7–12, 18–22, 27, 36, 66, 71, 73, 76, 78, 80–82, 89, 101–2, 105, 116–24, *123*
Plato 57, 122
polis 56–57, 61–64, *65*, 67, 77–79, 82, 118
power 15, 17, 31–33, 39, 44–48, 68, 79, 91, 95–97, 104, 117, 119, 123
primeval mound 36–37
Pseudo-Scylax 71, *72*
Ptolemaic Period 28, *30*
Punt (land of) 39
Puteoli 110, 120
pylon 35, 48
pyramid 35–39, 42, 48; *Pyramid Texts* xi, 35
Pytheas 80

rebirth 33–35, 37, 47
Red Sea 19, 39, 42–43, 80, 108–9
Rhine 20, 87, 90, 96
river 2–3, 17, 19–20, 27, 31–39, 43, 47, 54, 57, 66, 73–74, 87, 89–91, 96, 102, 105–7, 109, 117, 121
road 1, 3, 9, 38, 40, 89, 97–109, *99*, 120, 124
Rome 6, 10, 12–13, 15, 17–18, 20, 68, 81, 87, 90–91, 95, 97, 104–6, 110–11, 118, 120–21; Roman army 97, 106, 109; Roman citizenship 90, 123; Roman empire 13, 15, 20, 38, 68–69, 82, 87, 89–90, *94*, 95, 97–98, *99*, 104–6, 111, 117, 119, 123–24; Roman miles 102, 106

Sahara 14, 28, 95, 97
Sataspes 74
seafaring 19, 57, 69, 71, 111
season 9–10, 31–33, 38, 48, 78, 89, 98, 110
Seth 34, 45–47
ship 62, 67, 69–71, 75–76, 78–80, 87, 89, 102–3, 110
Sicily 71, 102, 110
Sinai 27, 31
space (concept of) x-xi, 3–5, 7–8, 11, 13, 18–20, 22, 31–32, 48, 61, 63–64, 67, 70, 73–74, 81, 101, 111, 116–20, 122, 124
Sparta 62, 66–68
Strabo 7–9, 74, 77, 95
Sudan 7, 14, 54, 120
Suez Canal 42–43
sun xi, 1, 4, 5, 31, 33–37, 47–48, 80, 103
sun-god 27, 35, 38
survey 7, 41–42, 103

Tabula Peutingeriana 104–5, 111, 120
temple 35–39, 43–44, 46, 48, 119
territory 1–3, 12, 17, 19–20, *29–30*, 31, 33, 35, 40, 48, 54, 56, 61–62, 64, 68, 77–78, 87–90, *88*, *92–93*, 95–97, 103–4, 106, 108–11, 116–18, 120–21
Thucydides x, 57, 68
time (concept of) x-xi, 1, 2, 5–7, 10–13, 15, *16*, 18, 20, 32, 36, 38, 42–43, 47, 63, 69–71, 74–77, 90, 101, 103, 107, 110, 117–20, 122–23
tomb 35–37, 39–40, 45, 48
topography 11, 35
trade 12–14, 17, 19–20, 48, 54–55, 64, 77–78, 108, 116–20
travel 1–3, 7–9, 12–15, 18–20, 28, 38–42, 48, 68–71, 73, 79–80, 89, 96–97, 101–5, 108–11, 116–20, 122
Trojan war x, 57, 63
Tyrrhenian Sea 90, 98, 120

Valley of the Kings 36
Vitruvius 10

wadi 1, 35, 41; Wadi Tumilat 43
warfare 12, 64, 116
water 1, 9–10, 14–15, 20, 27, 31–34, 36–40, 42–44, 46–48, 67, 69–71, 74, 76, 78, 81, 91, 98, 100, 109, 121–22

Western Desert 1, 4, 19, 27, 31, 116, 119
wind 1, 10, 14, 38, 69, 74–76, 103

Yam (land of) 40–41

For Product Safety Concerns and Information please contact our EU representative GPSR@taylorandfrancis.com
Taylor & Francis Verlag GmbH, Kaufingerstraße 24, 80331 München, Germany

www.ingramcontent.com/pod-product-compliance
Lightning Source LLC
Chambersburg PA
CBHW051751230426
43670CB00012B/2242